# MYTH
## of the
# BARRENS

## A Native Journey Through the Barren Lands of Canada

### BREN KOLSON

ESCHIA
BOOKS

The Publisher: Eschia Books Inc.

Library and Archives Canada Cataloguing in Publication

Kolson, Bren
Myth of the barrens / Bren Kolson.

ISBN 978-1-926696-07-2

1. Kolson, Bren.  2. Northwest Territories—Biography.
3. Tundras—Northwest Territories.  4. Métis  women—Biography.
I. Title.

FC4173.1.K64A3 2009        971.9'304092        C2009-905172-9

*Project Director and Editor:* Kathy van Denderen
*Cover Image:* Courtesy of Photos.com
*Photos*: Photographs by Bren Kolson

We acknowledge the support of the Alberta Foundation for the
Arts for our publishing program.

PC: 1

# Dedication

*For my daughter Kiera-Dawn Kolson, my parents Mary (nee Morrison) and Michael Kolson and for all family members. For Richard Black and Louison Drybones.*

*A special dedication for Frank MacMaster, Theresa Drybones, Noel Drybones, Jim Magrum, Henry Cadieux, Wilfred Smith, Judith Catholique and Lawrence Catholique.*

*And for June Magrum and family, Madeline Drybones, Eddy Drybones, Marlene and Aileen Drybones, Doris Cassaway, Mary Cassaway-Drybones, Johnny (J.C.) Catholique, Felix Lockhart, Ray Griffith, Pierre Catholique, Mary Cadieux, Ray Hamilton, Barb MacKenzie, Bill Carpenter.*

*For the bush pilots who took us in and out of the Barren Lands and the wildlife and game wardens who brought our Christmas mail and presents.*

*And for the men of the expedition, "A Traverse to the North West: (1977–78)."*

# Acknowledgements

MANY PEOPLE ARE INVOLVED IN THE EDITING AND THE pre- and post-production and publishing of a book, not only the author in writing the book. Involvement includes persons who were a part of the story 30 years ago, who may not be a part of, or in, our presence today. *Myth of the Barrens* began as a project to record the daily events of a way of life in a remote and isolated geography of the Barren Lands of the Northwest Territories. The book, written in a diary format, was to invite the reader into the landscapes of Aboriginal traditional life, becoming a way of the past, in the particular area of the Barren Lands where we lived, hunted, fished, trapped and survived.

I want to acknowledge Louison Drybones and Richard Black for providing me a once-in-a-lifetime unforgettable experience and for all you both taught me about how to live and survive a beautiful and spiritual region of the North and of the world. *Myth of the Barrens* is a realistic portrayal of surviving the Barren Lands and will always represent a historical documentation of a 20th-century Barren Land adventure.

I wish to acknowledge and thank my editor, Kathy van Denderen. I appreciated your excellent wealth of editing information. I enjoyed working with you because of your frank, jovial and wonderful personality to engage, involve and ensure the author was as satisfied as you were with the final product.

I want to thank my daughter, Kiera-Dawn Kolson, for her support throughout the years, for hearing many times "in a moment, Sweetie," because I was typing the last word in a sentence and the "moment" extended to two or three hours. I wish to acknowledge the friendly, brief commentary of my friend Lois Little who read the first 10 pages years ago when I thought I had a book. She said, "It's good, Bren. Really good." Subtly, a moment later, she said, "But…you might want to flesh it out a bit."

I want to thank the N.W.T Arts Council and the Canada Council for the Arts for the financial contributions much needed to complete my creative artistic project and commitment to ensure all northern artists have your support.

I wish for all persons to enjoy the read!

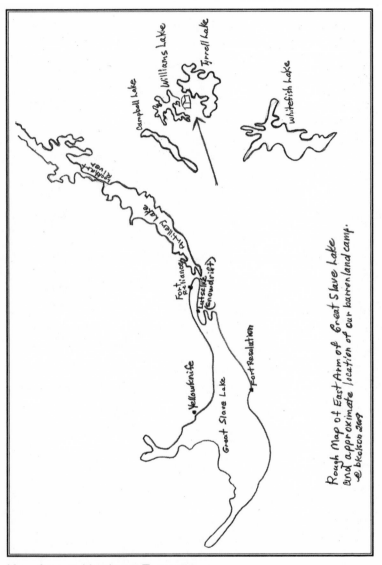

Map of area in Northwest Territories

# Contents

# Introduction
## Preview from a Carriole

THE SLEIGH DIPPED AT AN ANGLE FROM SIDE TO SIDE ON crunching ice and snow. The rhythm of the crooked sway sounded like a repeat of the words "in tandem." The eight dogs ran in tandem pulling the heavy load. There was nothing to do but take the ride, play word games with myself and sit in a frigid stare at the blackness of the night.

I repeated the words "in tandem, in tandem, in tandem" slowly and then faster until the words were a sleepy drawl in my mind. "Ninnn-tan-demmm, ninnn-tan-demmm, ninn-tan-demmm."

Curling in a fetal position in the carriole, deeply compacted in the Five-Star sleeping bag, helped me avoid chilled bones and the constant shiver of cold numbness. Rhythms rocked body, mind and soul in and out of black sleep. The canvas and caribou-skin fur-lined carriole was overlain with more white canvas and caribou-skin tarps for warmth. The hand-scraped hides once protected and sheltered huge bodies of bull caribou. The hides once breathed life. I breathed air invisible to my sight. The dogs ran the rocky and barren land my eyes could not see. Couched in my temporary home, I stared wide-eyed but saw nothing, because it was darker than black is blind.

It was the evening of the first day of our two-and-a-half-day journey from the Mary Francis River at the mouth of Williams Lake, the "big lake," on the Barren Lands of the Northwest Territories in December 1975. I did not know the land or land-marks, but Richard knew how to read the land like a map and how to direct the dogs toward our final destination of Fort Reliance on the east arm of Great Slave Lake. The time it took to travel by dog team depended on the strength of the dogs to pull the weight of the load.

Richard cursed at one of the dogs to turn left as he stood at the back of the sleigh. His words sounded like wisps of ghost words passing in the night air. I heard him but did not see him. There were no street lights to guide the trail.

"Where do words go?" I asked the night air.

Words go into darkness, with billions of other words spoken and yet to be spoken. Words said out loud can be words of hurt and sorrow; some are pretty words—colourful, descriptive words of beauty to tell someone or to write down. Words are meant to be believable, but some words are lies—not to be believed and are quite untrue.

Some people are afraid to experiment with words, afraid to think beyond the furthest possible expansion of expression. The experience I had on the Barren Lands was far removed from my existent lifestyle as a reporter and photojournalist. It was a re-identification, revelation and renewal of a similar lifestyle I had lived in an earlier period of my life.

There was silence when my mind voices ceased. A mind occupied prevents death by total refrigerated boredom. "I'm sure this has got to be darker and colder than Sam McGee's concept of hell," I thought. I coughed intentionally to hear my voice as it disappeared into the Barren Land air. It was a slow cough in a cool mist—off to join the mistress of coldness. The frozen cough sounded surrealistic, if surrealism has a sound. Coughing was one way to remind me of my existence and to ban boredom and insanity.

The sleigh continued its slow grind of incessant icy messages in an invisible wintry barren land, as it, too, jostled and endured the black snow and ice. The ominous trail buggy rocked in lullaby swing, entrancing me with miracles of pending warmth, but my brain continued to send monotone, biological messages: "Your toes and feet may soon lose feeling." My body was cold and numb, but the coldness and numbness were keeping me aware of my human existence.

"You good old feet, I should have treated you better. I should have given you a real bath instead of soapy, soppy, sponge baths. I should have pampered you with hot water, rather than water cooled too fast for comfort." I wiggled and wiggled my socks and moccasin-bound toes back and forth, back and forth, to regain sensation and free my toes from intended misery.

"You've done a lot of walking around the main camp at Williams Lake and to and from outpost camps. You have definitely leaned stealthily to scour sand-covered eskers, dug deep into autumn moss lining freezing lake shores, learned to manoeuvre hopping hummocks as if playing snakes and ladders, and felt the rough jut of rock and the smooth, hard-packed dirt of the Barren Land Precambrian Shield. You learned how to lift the weight of fresh-cut caribou meat and pails of fish and have hauled hulks of chipped ice."

My toes were fixed in a rhythmic motion back and forth, back and forth. The dogs pulled the load of survival. Survival: to continue to exist, to remain alive, to endure, to stay alive longer than the will to live. Life on the Barren Lands was a world of survival, to work hard and exist. The right of survival and existence depended on the kill: you must kill, and you must eat, or perish. The survivor must kill the animal, the bird, the fish and eat the berries and herbs and find drinkable water.

The land, air and water were the Master's guides, but Mother Earth provided the food, clothing and shelter. The land also could kill you if you broke a leg far from camp, if you misjudged the thickness of ice or if no caribou passed by the camp. The land dictated the balance between life and death, existence and survival. The Master and Mother Earth showed me and taught me what was weak and must die, what was strong and could survive, what gave willingly and what did not.

The Great Spirit of the land, sky and water permitted Louison Drybones, Richard Black and me the right to survive the Barren Lands, but there is a process to survival. Specific items we carried in the sleigh ensured our survival.

Various sizes of hand-sewn canvas bags, carefully packed and positioned to preserve space in the carriole, held the load of survival: axe, hatchet, small homemade barrel stove, small canvas tent, well-used and sharp—in case of a sudden kill— knives and penknives as well as files and whetstones. One canvas sack contained candles in small plastic tubes, an aluminum tea pail blackened from fire and a larger pot for drinking and wash water, when fresh water was available. If not, ice chipped from a frozen lake, river or stream and melted over a fire was our source of water. The sack also held tea towels, face towels and toilet paper.

In another larger canvas bag tied with a rope were smaller hand-sewn canvas pouches individually filled with loose oatmeal, salt, pepper, baking powder, tea, powdered milk, coffee, brown sugar, flour for bannock and frozen lard and butter. Leftover chocolate bars from the fall grub box not chewed by mice or Richardson squirrels were a store-bought treat, not a treat from the land: drymeat was a treat from the land.

There were two cans of frozen peaches to be opened with a hunting knife and melted over a morning fire for the added taste of fruit, in a land where no fruit trees, and few other trees, grow. In a large bag, considered most important, was the fur from animals caught during the fall and winter trapping season: red fox, white fox, cross fox, silver or blue fox. I used the bag as a leaning post.

At the back, where Richard guided the sleigh and dogs, in a large canvas bag were a dozen frozen fish for our meals and for dog feed. Dried caribou meat to be eaten with salted lard or butter was in a separate bag. Bannock would be cooked before each meal in a kneeling position in the tent. Richard's 303 and .22 rifles, tent pegs and various sizes of traps were also packed at the back of the sleigh. His shell bag crisscrossed his outer caribou-skin parka.

A canvas tent lined the bottom of the sleigh, covered with caribou-skin hides to sleep on when the tent was set up in the snow for the evening. A small stove owned the crook of the curve at the front of the sleigh. It bumped and banged a floppy rhythm at the end of my frozen feet. Clothes in packsacks and duffle bags were positioned along the inner sides of the sleigh, on top of our sleeping bags.

If there was room, and only if there was room, were some personal items for warmth, not fashion or fad. I hid my journal among personal clothing because I was told the sleigh would be too heavy if I took frivolous items not necessary for survival. The camera film and the few sketches I drew were also hidden among my clothes. The words I wrote and the photographs I took were too dear to be left for an illiterate bear musing the silence of the cabin to pick at and destroy when looking for something to eat.

When the dog-team journey began, I snuggled in the sleeping bags. Richard loosely arranged the caribou hides and canvases over the entire load and roped me in the sleigh to shape and fix the position of the load. I was not roped in entirely. I could move enough to feel sensation in my bum. It was a heavy load for the dogs to pull, but the dogs were strong and powerful and pulled the load with a slow ease. When we left Mary Francis River at Williams Lake, I didn't think I would be sitting in a sleigh for most of the day.

I wanted to get out of the sleigh and move around, but Richard wanted to travel a required number of miles per day. I did not ask to be removed from the sleigh. I endured, as my eyes sensed and nose breathed the unseen ink of blackness. I breathed in and out, in and out of the frosted scarves. The temperature was well below –45°F.

Through the thin slit in the scarves I wound around my neck and face, my eyes blurred with water from the passing cold wind's whip at the sudden turn on the trail. I blinked fast to prevent my lower eyelashes from freezing to the upper lashes. My back banged against the fur bag and sleigh spine when the bag moved too far out of position left or right. I squirmed in a monotonous zone of discomfort until the bag of fur hides righted into position.

A tingling sensation re-entered the flesh on the backside of my body. My lower back ached. I resumed ultimate patience in an inanimate land of cold and raven black. I snuggled deeper into my self-made temporary womb, waiting for the sleigh world above me to stop.

# BOOK ONE

September 1975 to December 1975

>—I—◆>—O—<◆—I—<

THE JOURNALS I KEPT OF BARREN LAND LIFE WERE written in seven-day periods, beginning in September 1975 and concluding in December 1975 and beginning again in August 1977 and concluding in January 1978. There are no entries for periods I did not write in my diary. I wrote the two books in diary format and took over 300 photographs. I wrote 14 poems about the Barren Lands and drew a few sketches. I also saved the Barren Land letters written by Richard Black to me during my relationship with Fort Reliance and the Barren Lands as well as the letters written to me by Louison Drybones.

The documentation I researched didn't include any written information by a northern Métis woman. I believe I am the first Métis woman to write about the Barren Lands. The experiences of a non-Aboriginal man, a Métis woman and a Dene elder living on the Barren Lands of the Northwest Territories in the mid-1970s was a unique situation to write about.

When I first saw the Barren Lands in August 1975, it was indeed a cold, rainy and windy day. I was invited by Richard Black to fly in the DC-3 aircraft from Fort Reliance on the east arm of Great Slave Lake to Williams Lake on the Barren Lands. I had met him in Yellowknife and visited him at Fort Reliance during the summer months. Richard, who was from Beloit, Wisconsin, was a slight man, 5 feet 7 inches, and not hefty or large-boned, with blond hair. He was a strong, good-looking man of part Norwegian descent who took an interest in living on the land and learned to love it. He flew to the Barren Lands to live with a 67-year-old Chipewyan elder, Louison Drybones, to learn to hunt and trap. Richard and I had talked about me going on the land in the winter, but he thought it would be too cold.

My first flight to the Barrens was to accompany Richard to bid him farewell and to see where he was going to trap for the winter. In late August 1975, the plane flew an hour before landing on rough, frothing, whitecaps on the shores of Williams Lake. Friends on the plane helped Richard unload food, fuel, materials, sleigh and dogs. The items were placed randomly on lichen, moss and rock. Bright summer colours were transformed by the cold wind and rain into stark autumn colours. Richard was right about the Barren Land cold. I was chilled standing on the shore before our departure.

When I left Richard standing on the Barrens, I returned to Yellowknife to work at *The Native Press* as a reporter and photojournalist. I reported on the Mackenzie Valley Pipeline Inquiry, also known as the Berger Inquiry, which travelled to communities in the North to hold formal and informal hearings about oil and gas pipelines.

In September 1975, my decision to fly to the Barren Lands to live was encouraged by many elders who spoke at the informal community hearings. What better source of reference than from living legends? The Dene, Métis and Inuvialuit elders gave explicit details about making, repairing and setting nets, about sewing clothing from animal skins, about fishing, hunting and trapping techniques, and about gathering and preparing berries and herbs for a variety of medicinal and household purposes. Encyclopedias could be written about Aboriginal traditional knowledge and wisdom of the elders of the Mackenzie Valley.

I bought supplies in early September 1975 for my flight to the Barren Lands. Was I prepared for no electricity, no shopping at grocery stores for food, no indoor toilet, no money and no automatic clothes washer, I wondered?

Noel Drybones was Louison Drybones' half brother. Noel's son, Eddy, agreed to share a chartered plane from Fort Reliance to Campbell Lake and Williams Lake. Noel's family hunted and trapped at Campbell Lake, north of Williams Lake.

Eddy's wife, Doris, helped me choose which supplies to buy to live where the men joked was "no-woman's land."

## ᛘ᛭ September 4, 1975–September 11, 1975 ᛘ᛭

I FLEW TO THE BARREN LANDS FEELING AS IF I WAS a female version of John the Baptist going forth into the wilderness: a soul survivor. On the trip, the view from the plane's cockpit showed a different geography than what I saw on my first visit to the Barren Lands a month earlier. The clean white flow of Parry Falls signalled the approach to the Barren Lands. The plane flew over Artillery Lake en route to Campbell Lake. There were sparse trees, small long eskers, a blend of small rivers and every colour of autumn on bush, lichen and moss. Light-brown colours looked pasted on patches of grey rock. From the view looking down, 500 feet above the land, the drag of the plane looked as though someone was pulling a collage of various colours in roller-coaster fashion across the sky.

"He's probably hunting caribou," Eddy said, leaning his face against the window.

"Who?" I asked.

"My father," he replied.

I looked out the window to see three caribou loping across the land in slow cinematic motion.

The caribou looked huge. Eddy pointed to his father, then to the direction of the caribou. The pilot circled twice and dipped the plane's wing to indicate the direction of the caribou. Eddy's father waved his gun in the air in recognition he understood which direction the caribou were travelling.

In 10 minutes, the plane landed on Campbell Lake. My second observation of the Barren Lands was how one minute it could be warm and sunny, and the next minute, the sky was cloudy with lashing rain.

When I half stepped, half fell from the height of the open plane door, I didn't think the water would be as cold as it was. The lake water was freezing. I should have listened to Eddy and not been eager to help unload supplies for Noel and Eddy's family winter trapping season.

Two dogs chained inside the belly of the plane didn't want to jump into the water. It was doggy instinct; the last, languid, sultry days of summer were over, and the coming winter meant many days of hard work. In the distance on an esker was a stick-built plywood tent frame where Noel and his family lived. Because of the mid-afternoon fading light, the pilot wanted to leave quickly for Williams Lake. The weather was cold, but boarding the plane to travel to Williams Lake gave cause to thaw my freezing feet.

Eddy and I continued the plane ride to Williams Lake. He would later take the plane back to Campbell Lake where he would remain to trap with his parents, his wife and young daughter. The plane circled the main camp at Williams Lake. I saw a neatly organic arrangement: the cabin, with a washtub, saws and clothes hanging on its outer walls; a wooden sawhorse; a wood pile; dogs tied to one side of the cabin; a food stage on the other side of the cabin on a low hill; and a small lake in another direction in front of the larger Williams Lake.

A light blue smoky mist cured meat hanging on a homemade wooden meat rack. A nearby table was used for cutting the meat. An overturned canoe was in the bushes near the dogs. An outdoor toilet stood alone, as did the ribbed shell of a sleigh. A line of wire in a triangle stretched from the cabin to a pole on the hill and back around the cabin to another pole.

Richard stood near a triangular fish stage, one arm above his forehead to shade the sun for a view of the approaching airplane. The plane landed at a different location than in August when the plane took Richard to Louison's main Barren Land camp. Although the plane was set close to the bush, I had to walk in cold water once we deplaned. The water was warmer at Williams Lake. Richard walked to the plane around a hill through bushes. He was surprised to see me because it was not a pre-arranged decision for me to live on the land with him and Louison. While the pilot and Eddy drank tea in the cabin, Richard and I went for a walk, to talk about me staying, or not staying, on the Barrens. Louison was at an outpost camp. After discussing the pros and cons of life on the Barren Lands, it was decided I would stay.

We completed the ritual of unloading the plane. The utter loneliness I felt was overwhelming as the plane frayed the whitecaps and flew into the blue, sunny sky. I never heard such quiet, except when I first went to Fort Reliance in early 1975. It was so beautiful and peaceful; I thought I was in heaven.

The first lesson of survival was "glamour does not live on the Barren Lands." Hard work is the master of survival! It was hard work carrying heavy boxes for three-quarters of a mile when I hadn't exercised—ever. Richard and I relentlessly walked the bush path, past a burnt-out patch of trees, past a small lake and around a hill, before dumping the boxes on the ground near the cabin. I soon realized there was no telephone in case of an emergency, no vehicle to transport heavy meat carcasses and no return to civilization until the land was hard and snow-packed for dogs to travel on.

The first evening on the Barren Lands, I saw the sun slowly set over "the big lake," as Louison called Williams Lake, but the night was not dark. The task of gathering wood and small pieces of dry kindling began in the early evening. It became one of my daily rituals.

Gathering wood wasn't a difficult task, but walking the nearby hills and eskers to gather wood chips for kindling fuelled my imagination with childhood boogeyman stories. I saw Barren Land gophers skid into a small sandy hole as I stood to look at the grove of burnt trees. I wondered if a forest fire had burned the trees, but there were no forests on the Barren Lands. I learned Louison intentionally burned part of the grove for later use in the winter when it was too cold to travel greater distances to find wood. The burnt trees would eventually turn into dry wood he could chop down and saw. Huge rolling logs of dry wood found during the winter would be hauled by dog teams to the main campsite. A boat was used to haul wood from nearby small islands before the waters froze. Wood was one of the most important items of survival on the Barren Lands.

On a third trip to gather wood and kindling, I felt an eerie, creepy feeling as though someone was watching me. I shivered and hurried back to the main camp.

Another daily ritual was meal preparation. It took time to cook a meal because there were no stove knobs to turn on a burner and control the heat. The heat of the burning wood had to be just right before a meal could be cooked. An alternate source of heat was the Coleman stove, but it was rarely used. My first meal on the Barren Lands was macaroni and cheese, Kam and boiled cranberries. I surveyed the cabin as I ate and asked Richard questions about the cabin and about Louison. I was informed the main room in the cabin was a 7- × 12-foot single room, and it had been used many times by hunters and trappers since the 1930s. There were reminders of earlier trapping days and of previous tenants, who had carved words or initials on the inside logs of the outer storage room.

The cabin was habitable, affordable and suitable for living. The outer porch of three walls was attached to the main inner cabin. When the outer partition door of the storage-porch was opened into the cabin, a person stepped down one step onto old logs and a weathered plywood and part dirt floor. The second entry door to the main cabin was visible from any angle in the outer porch area. In the outer porch, two windows were strategically positioned for a view of all directions. The window's glass was covered with hard, clear, all-weather plastic. No curtains hung on the windows to hide an intrusive gaze because there was no one around to look into the windows.

On the walls were a variety of necessities for Barren Land survival, particularly the guns, caribou-hide shell bags, heavy-duty scrub brushes, rope, handsaws and a crosscut saw. Axes and boxes of miscellaneous material lay in different piles under a table built the length of the outer cabin room. Atop a huge, thick wooden barrel lid sat a large, round, heavy metal basin holding freshly slaughtered caribou. Flour bags, sugar and other dry goods were positioned variably on homemade wooden shelves. The downward slanting shelves looked to topple at any minute.

The cabin, the clothes and the land all had a distinctive smell. The smell was fresh, clean, unspoiled and gave an aura of being undisrupted. On the land, there were no foreign smells of a city, no car spinning rubber on asphalt, no smells of medicine from a hospital, no smells of intoxication from an open bar door, no smoky smell of burning garbage or smell of rotting food from a garbage dumpster on a hot summer's afternoon. Nor was there foul language expelled from the mouth of an angry person, no exotic or illicit shame of person, no pushing or shoving and no graveyards or gravestones to invoke sadness. There was only the scent of fresh, of clean, and a pureness I thought surely must be God.

I didn't think, and I didn't realize, I was invading the two men's privacy until it was bedtime. I slept on one bed, and Richard slept on the other bed, but I wondered how three people were going to sleep in the small cabin?

were played on me or I would have freaked. In a languid mood, I observed and thought about silence. I asked myself: What is silence?

I concluded silence is an ominous time without action. Silence is a space in time, but space and time are in the family of silence. Silence cannot be counted by a clock if no clock is ticking, because silence cannot be calculated without numbers. Who has calculated silence, except by using words and numbers? Silence absorbs time but shows no sign of its absorption. Silence has been forever, without sound, taste or smell and without feeling, emotion or thought. Silence is the essence of still, of hush, of spiritual contentment.

On November 2, I baked bannock and raisin tarts. The grey clouds always amazed me. Wisps of even brush strokes were painted across the sky. I was day-dreaming when I heard Louison's voice yell, "Whoa!" I gathered my bedding and moved to the caribou-skin tent.

After lunch Louison harnessed his dogs. I didn't know whether he was going back to an outpost camp or was going to gather wood. One dog escaped the harness and was running free around the yard. When Louison caught him, he gave him the worst beating. He held the dog by the collar so it couldn't escape and beat the dog with a chain. It couldn't run anywhere in the limited space.

I yelled for him to stop, and he finally heard me and stopped beating the dog. I may not have agreed with Louison's treatment of his dogs, but I couldn't change what he thought about his dogs or how he trained his dogs from pups to become sled dogs. Louison knew he had to show his dogs who the master was, or the dogs would become totally uncontrollable.

On the other hand, Richard was a gentler master. He whipped a dog if he thought the dog needed it, while swearing at it, but not with a chain and very seldom in a vicious manner. He would pet and talk to his dogs sometimes, but he, too, ensured the dogs knew who was master.

I went back to cooking my bannock and turned it over in the frying pan on the barrel stove. For a second time in one day, I heard, "Whoa!" It was Richard. We drank tea, and as I was cooking for him, we heard the dogs in quite a raucous. We went outdoors, thinking Louison had returned from hauling wood, but we remembered he went to one of his outpost camps. We were surprised to see Eddy Drybones leading his dog team to rest by the woodpile. During the afternoon we talked to Eddy about his trapping year, his parents, whether it would be a wealthy or a poor trapping season and whether or not the caribou migrated to Campbell Lake. He said there were plenty of caribou but not many trapped animals.

Late in the morning of the next day, the three of us walked around the hill where the plane, Eddy and I had first landed in September. The men looked for rabbit tracks, but instead, we saw clusters of ptarmigan feeding on willows 200 feet away.

The two men joked I couldn't hit a can 100 yards away so probably wouldn't be able to hit a ptarmigan. Eddy had a new .22 rifle with a dynamite scope. I shot two ptarmigan, one in the neck. How's that for an aim? Maybe it was because I could see through the vee and post and wasn't shooting with a .22 rifle with a bent vee and post on it. I was surprised to see Eddy pluck the feathers off the warm bird's breast while it still had a twinge of life in it. He just left the bird's breast feathers on the snow on the lake.

"Eeee-you! The heartlessness," I thought.

He said it was easier to pluck a bird when it was still warm and not frozen. What is it about men and animals on the Barren Lands? No respect, no dignity to allow the animal to die before cutting into caribou or defeathering birds. As Richard said, "What's the big deal? It's already dead! Are you going to cook them for supper?"

"Eeee-you! Do it yourself," I thought. Yes, I cooked the birds for supper.

Eddy hauled wood to the camp. When the men were gone for another long haul of wood, I took a bath, with towels hung over the windows for privacy. The men came back earlier than expected and banged and banged on the door, calling for me to open the door. I am a slow dresser but dressed as quickly as I could, but not fast enough, because both men said it was freezing cold. "We'll open the door whether you like it or not," the men warned after waiting half an hour. I finally opened the door, once clothed. It was cold outside, but what happened to macho strength of big tough Barren Land men?

We enjoyed the evening playing cards. Richard lost a case of shells to Eddy, and I won a few stick matches. Eddy was the big winner though, winning extra single shells from Richard hours after I was out of the game.

## 🦌 November 7, 1975–November 13, 1975 🦌

ON NOVEMBER 11, REMEMBRANCE DAY, I WROTE:

> I thought about poppies and white crosses. I thought about the wars of the world and, as many people have, wondered why there couldn't be peace in the world. I understand the dominant group wants to take what the minority group has, for "the sake of the take." It's happening here in the Northwest Territories without guns, over oil and gas, and the balance is whether Aboriginal people who have lived here on the land forever will have control of Aboriginal lands.

A beautiful sunset on the calm waters of Great Slave Lake

I am here on the land, and I see the spiritual beauty. It will be destroyed if things are not planned properly, or if multinational companies and governments have no vested interest to "give a little more" than take, take, take, as in the past.

The attitude of imperialist, colonialist ideology is still present in the North. Aboriginal people of the world are not allowed to have control over ancestral landscapes heritage: land for survival. Guns, war and death are done in the name of the children of the future.

I think the spirits of the land will always be here to protect future Aboriginal generations—no matter how many wars men fight. Aboriginal people have existed throughout all wars and will continue to live after people fighting wars are no more. The Barren Lands need to be preserved in case the world becomes so advanced it loses certain spiritual senses of the beautiful essence in, and all about, the land. I think it's as close as one human being can understand God on the earth. One day, the whiteman collective will survive by learning what the Aboriginal people have known for millenniums— but not any day soon.

At the end of the week, when I walked to a nearby hill to check traps in a one-mile radius around the campsite, I saw the bait was stolen. Richard trapped two white fox. I cut wood and sewed huge caribou-hide moccasin insulators. The large pieces of sewed caribou hide covered two pairs of moccasins and resembled gigantic furry snowshoes. My feet are forever cold.

We couldn't sleep because the dogs barked and barked. Richard went to see what the fuss was about. I think it is Brandy, the cleverest dog I've ever known, playing his disappearing act. I've seen Richard tie Brandy's collar so tight he was almost choking him, and still, he slipped his collar.

I think Brandy slipped his collar and made like a sultry night wolf on the prowl. Maybe he has a wolf girlfriend. He's a stinker and he's smart. He enjoys the freedom of the nightlife, but I call him Mr. Skulk and Sneak. He slips his collar, and when he sees Richard coming, he runs back to his dog post among the clan and lays down, pretending he was never loose in the first place. I think he's also helping himself to a feed of meat hanging on the meat rack, but I never could find teeth marks to accuse him.

When Richard came back into the cabin, the raucous was on again. It took three times before Richard figured out what Brandy was doing. Richard swore at the dog and warned him he would lose his doggy manhood if he slipped his collar again. Brandy understood and cried a meek whine, seeking reprieve.

Snow finally came to the Barren Lands. Before I crawled into my sleeping bag I saw light wind wisp snow in frantic fashion all around the cabin site and distant land. Although it had snowed earlier in the fall, this was now a heavier snowfall.

## 🦌 November 14, 1975–November 20, 1975 🦌

THE SNOW DID NOT CEASE FALLING. THE WIND BEAT great swirls of mini tornadoes around the land. Richard harnessed the dogs to the sleigh to go find wood. A rabbit lost a toe in one trap he checked, but no fox were caught in nearby traps.

Louison came back from an old outpost camp at the Hanbury River. It was a long trip by dog team both to and from the camp. He was gone five days and trapped three white fox. He considered the fox to be "blue," suitable for auction, but not considered prime fur. As he ate a mid-afternoon lunch, he told stories and said he did not think the fur was ready for trapping. He didn't see or shoot caribou and didn't see tracks or signs of caribou. He set traps in a radius from the Hanbury River camp to his outpost camp on Williams Lake. He talked about seeing many tracks of animals, though. If lucky, he said he would trap wolves, wolverine or ermine with a Number One trap and not the larger Number Three trap. The size of the animal dictated what size trap was used to trap the animal. If the trappers were lucky, the reward was a cinnamon or grizzly bear hide to be sold at auction to buy food and supplies for the next year's trapping season.

The fur must be removed from a trapped animal. It is the fur the trapper wants and makes money from, and there is a lesson to be learned about skinning animals. It was a lesson I didn't want to learn and was one of the grossest scenes I've witnessed.

Louison sat on the edge of his bed in the cabin and tied a rope to a drying rack attached to the inverted "V" wooden struts of the ceiling. If I had known what it was used for, I wouldn't have hung my clean clothes on it. He swung a rope over a drying rack pole.

The rope dangled in front of him. He tied one of the legs of the white fox to the dangling rope. I saw all, sitting on the bed across from the man who skinned fox. With a penknife he cut the white fox near the bum and up the inside of the legs. The cut was like the letter "U" from the inside of the right leg to the inside and to the end of the left leg. He cut the feet off the skin. He turned the fox around and pulled the skin off the fox downward. He used the penknife to razor the fur off the fox, pulling the fur over the fox's head to the nose. UGGGH!

The white fox fur hide hung by the tip of the nose. The bloody skeleton hung upside down by one leg on a rope. Louison cut the nose from the red nose flesh, leaving only a carcass. It was gross to see the outline of the raw rib cage. I never thought about what trappers do to get the fur or the process used to collect the fur.

It literally gave me shivers and made my stomach queasy. I thought I was going to get sick, but I held it together despite what I saw. Louison must have skinned hundreds of animals in his life. Would I, too, have to skin an animal if one was in my traps? I didn't know whether I could, or could not, skin animals. I prayed no animal would step into the traps I set.

Louison was very good about cleaning the work area, and no blood dripped from the animals because of the clean cut. He untied the carcass and put it somewhere outside. I say "somewhere," because I never saw the carcasses or where the carcasses were put. I know he never fed the carcasses to the dogs either, because dogs will not eat raw fox flesh. My guess was he had a place he put the rest of the fox. But really, who had to know? He thoroughly washed his hands with soap and scraped his cuticles and nails with a small scrub brush.

It was very difficult to swallow my food at supper. It was more difficult to chew the caribou meat. Louison was talkative, and I wondered if he guessed my nausea. I focused on the story he was telling, to avoid vomiting all over the cabin. The original storyteller said, "One time I lived with the Eskimos at the Hanbury River. Me just a young man then. Lots of people at the Hanbury River then. Eskimo eat like this!"

He took a piece of meat with his fingers, put it to his mouth and, with a knife in the other hand, cut the meat close to his lips. I thought he might cut his lips, but he didn't.

I watched him use his bare hands to pretend to eat raw meat. "That's the way Eskimo eat," he said. "Now, don't eat like that. Eat with knife and fork. That time trapped with Jim and June Magrum. You know her husband a nice guy. He always laughed. He gone now. Me and June Magrum good friends."

I just about vomited because it was the first time I saw a red raw animal's skeleton, and the animals he had just skinned looked like raw meat he was pretending to eat. Many people will never understand Louison's way of life. Trapping was all he knew; he never flinched or thought it was something he should not do for a living. It was his right, to choose and decide to continue his historical Aboriginal right to the land.

I thought about Louison's stories and the Aboriginal traditional knowledge lost when he would someday go to another dimension or somewhere in the sky. Pages of history will be lost without him. I asked him what it was like living at the Hanbury River. He answered, "That time, lots of fur. Everybody trapped that time. Jim Magrum had a big house at the Hanbury River and lots of kids then. All your life trapped there and then go to Edmonton to sell fur.

"Boy, oh, boy, stay in King Edward Hotel. Just like Caribou Skin Hotel. Big Joe Nelson and lots of trappers were there that time. Just drink, drink, drink, for one whole week! Fancy hotel—spend lots of money that time. Ho, lots of women that time too. Me never stayed in hotel like that kind—but Big Joe Nelson and other trappers said, 'Come on. Come on. You buy first round.' They told me I buy the first drink, and I told him, 'Me a good man. Me go to church. Me don't drink.'

"And Big Joe Nelson told me, 'Come on, you son of a bitch. You trapped more white fox than all us trappers together. You buy the first drink for everybody.' So I buy first drink, and we drink, drink, drink, for one whole week and never paid for nothing...drink, drink, drink, all the time. Never saw so many whitemen that time. Too many whitemen that time. Skin just like flour. White like that. Stayed in Edmonton a long time that time and then come back to the Hanbury River and trapped some more."

I asked him what year it was he trapped at the Hanbury River and he said "Must be…1954…long time ago."

I asked him how long he trapped on the Barren Lands, and he said, "Must be…all my life. Trapped from 18 years. Some friends, in Snowdrift, say make lots of money trapping when I'm 16. So I go with them and trap, trap all my life. Lots of stuff at Hanbury River. Some people say gold there too. Me see something not look like gold. I know where, but never tell nobody."

I didn't question him further, and the cabin was silent, except for the sound of snapping sparks in the old, burnt-out barrel stove. Years later, diamonds were found on the Barren Lands.

The full moon illuminated the snow, hills, eskers, lakes, canvas on carriole, the meat-drying rack—all looked painted with ice frost and moon-shaped snow sparklers. The dogs were covered in moon glow. I wished I had a camera for night photography, but the picture remains only in my mind.

On November 15, I walked the land with Richard's Minolta camera. I heard the wind's howl in my ears. It sounded like the voices of a million lost souls echoing cries in my head. The wind made interesting sounds in the hollow of my ears, and new sounds I heard depended on which direction my head was turned.

Back at the camp, I lit the stove to dispel chilled bones and read. Louison checked nearby traps. He held two white fox. One fox was not in good condition, with a blue-black colour under its chin. Louison showed it to me and said the fox must have been hungry. Richard and I sawed wood before we retired for the evening to the Caribou Skin Hotel.

The topic of conversation was the same: where to go next on the land; when to ready for the next journey; how many fox would step into one of the men's traps; how much longer to stay on the land before returning to Fort Reliance or Snowdrift. The discussion also continued on how well the dogs were performing, how many and which dogs to take, whether to begin a new line to trap, and what the weather was like on the last journey to an outpost camp.

Richard read about John Hornby and Edgar Christian who died on the Barren Lands near Warden's Grove at the Thelon River. The men died because they miscalculated the caribou migration, and they starved to death. The younger Englishman, Edgar Christian, left a diary in the pot-belly stove.

While Richard read, Louison sewed black fur around the outer rim of a parka hood. When Louison said he was going to an outpost camp the following day, Richard said he would make the journey to his outpost camp at Tyrrell Lake in a northerly direction from the main camp. I asked to go with him to his outpost camp. He said no. I will be alone on the Barren Lands, again.

Joseph Burr (J.B.) Tyrrell (1858–1957), a geologist, cartographer and mining consultant, was employed by the Geological Survey of Canada and led two expeditions in 1893 and 1894 to survey the Barren Lands, and in 1885 and 1900 he surveyed lands between Great Slave Lake and Hudson Bay.

The next morning, Louison went in an easterly direction. Richard said the wind was too strong to go to his outpost camp and instead decided to set traps in a westerly direction from the main cabin. My greatest feat for the day was to make peanut butter cookies. It was a movie scene based on a comedy of errors. Get your popcorn, the movie is about to begin.

The setting: A rustic Christmas card, picture-perfect snow-bound cabin on the Barren Lands.

The theme: Will our cook succeed in baking perfect, yummy-tasting peanut butter cookies, or will small, round, burnt peanut butter cookies usurp her baking abilities?

The plot (which did thicken): A sweet young thing in blue jeans and mukluks, wearing four sweaters, mixes a flurry of ingredients in an old, stained plastic bowl. (The camera pans the cookery to focus on what Little Miss Suzy Homemaker is preparing.)

The truth: The batter was made. The stove was warmed to a "guessed" temperature. The question is, will the batter form a cookie? Miss Suzy Homemaker dabs small chunks of batter onto the frying pan and, and…it totally melts. The batter must be too thin. The cookie maker is seen dumping two cups of oatmeal into the batter to thicken it.

Moulding it with her nimble fingers, the batter begins to grow and grow and grow…like the BLOB…into a GREAT BIG CRUMBLE GLOB. Now, she guesses, it shouldn't melt so fast. Who really cared if peanut butter cookies become disguised as peanut butter squares? Nicely shaped and well-rounded spoonfuls of oatmeal peanut butter glob dough are transferred from plastic bowl to frying pan. Miss Homemaker is staring at the pan, waiting for the blob of dough to melt. It doesn't melt; however, it didn't quite cook either. It kind of cooked while in the frying pan, just sitting in the big black frying pan. Soon, little parts of the round blob of dough begin to show signs of cracks.

Miss Suzy, in an elated frenzy and clapping her hands to the sides of her face with mouth wide open, realizes there is only one solution: keep plopping blob dough onto the frying crumble.

And then, the unexpected happened. The frying crumble grew and grew and grew until it became one gigantic oatmeal frying peanut butter cookie the size of the large, black, cast-iron frying pan. "Oh, well," Miss Suzy sighs, "better a peanut butter bannock than a braised peanut butter batter." She looks at the sympathetic audience gleefully and says, "Say that five times, fast!" In the meantime, I took the dough blob out of the frying pan, added a few more ingredients to bring it to a thicker consistency and made 20 little peanut butter bannocks and dumped the rest of the crumble, which looked like peanut butter anyway, back into the peanut butter can.

In a cooking mood, I made cranberry jam the way Louison taught me. He melted half a pound of lard in the big frying pan, sprinkled salt in it, and, when it began to sizzle, dumped in enough cranberries to cover the lard and fill the pan. The lard cooked the cranberries.

He dumped in a cup of sugar and stirred it. He let the cranberries pop and cook until the mixture was cooked into a cranberry sauce. It tasted delicious and froze when placed in the outer room. When we wanted cranberry jam, we spooned the lard and cranberries out of the jars and fried it again. The jam never burned.

Next on the menu was a caribou roast, wrapped in tin foil after spicing it with onion salt, garlic salt, pepper and salt. I threw the wrapped meat into the fire belly of the stove to cook. We would have broiled or burnt caribou roast for supper with peanut butter bannock for dessert. If the roast burnt, I could throw it back into the fire, and no one would know the difference. If it didn't burn and was cooked well, I would still throw it back into the fire to cook to perfection. I was having fun in my little cooking corner of the world, until a most curious thing happened. I heard a sleigh but didn't hear the voice of the sleigh's driver. I wondered if I was becoming a stoned bush bunny on my own cooking high.

I listened but heard no voice or voices. I went to the outer room window and saw Louison's dogs lying on the ground but no Louison in sight. I waited, thinking he would come into the cabin, but he didn't. Twenty minutes later when I looked again, I saw the small frame of a man bobbing across Williams Lake. I watched Louison walk past the shoreline, before he walked the path leading to the cabin. When he finally arrived, he told me what had happened.

He was setting a trap on the other side of Williams Lake and was about to jump into the sleigh, when the dogs jumped and were off. He couldn't run fast enough to catch or to stop the dogs. He walked for over an hour across Williams Lake to the cabin. Then, he grabbed a couple of chains and beat the dogs. Some dogs weren't expecting the lash and yelped suddenly, other dogs cowered and tried to run in all directions to evade the lash of the wild man's swing. He was so angry that I was afraid he would swing at me. I went into the cabin.

It seemed a long, long time, and I thought he was finished the beating, but when I looked out the window, he was still beating his dogs. I tried to yell at him to stop, but I don't think he heard me. I never wanted to try to physically stop him because of the way he swung so wildly. I wasn't going to be beaten with a chain by someone with wild eyes who didn't know how to stop because he was somewhere else in his mind. He finally stopped lashing and unharnessed the dogs, which then lay down to lick swollen wounds. I resolved it was his business, and I didn't have a say in his business.

Domestic dogs are pampered pets. The master buys pet food, feeds the pet, provides a safe shelter, cleans up after the pet, bathes the pet, plays with, cares for and spoils the pet. Sled dogs are bred for one purpose—to work. Most work dogs bred and trained to pull a sleigh are born and live in a rural, remote and wild environment.

A dog trained to pull a sleigh may eat every second day depending on the availability of food. It doesn't have shelter and usually lives outdoors in all types of weather. If the master of work dogs allowed the dog to be pampered, it would not work, and if the dogs don't work in a sleigh, the master would not survive the land. Sled dogs are a necessary part of Barren Land life, and it's the only life a sled dog knows. If the dog did not listen to the master, it would form a pack of wild dogs, as domestic dogs can also do, and cause chaos and even death to its master.

Richard wasn't back from his camp, and I was afraid. It was an uneasy and uncomfortable feeling not knowing how Louison would react after he had beaten the dogs. I didn't know who he was when he beat his dogs. From what I saw and knew of him from living on the Barrens, he seemed to be a good man. It was also very difficult to assume I could give an elder heck or advice about what he was doing. I also didn't want to make enemies with one of the only two other human beings on the Barrens. I was learning a way of life he lived for 69 years, and who was I to try to change it when I was new at learning how to live on the land, and he was teaching me?

When Louison came into the cabin, he acted as though nothing had happened. I wasn't in a talkative mood, so I ate and went to the caribou-skin tent to write in my diary by candlelight.

The evening was cool with a thin cloud cover crossing the moon, and a light fog covered the land. I imagined the fog as a phantom cloud slithering over the land as a shadow but was quickly covered by moon glow when it disappeared as fast as it came. I snuggled in my sleeping bag, reading and occasionally dozing off. The candle burned low, but the wood stove was still heated. I placed the candle on an old baking powder can, and it sat haphazardly on spruce boughs. I dozed off, and the candle burned itself out. The remaining hot wax crawled down the inside of the baking powder can, crept onto a bed of spruce boughs just beneath my sleeping bag. The wax rolled toward the damper of the stove, where coals still heat the wood stove, and began to burn. The spruce needles near the bottom of my sleeping bag were burning. If I had fallen into a deep sleep, I would have burned alive inside the caribou-skin tent.

Because God loves me, at one moment when I opened my eyes, I saw burning spruce boughs at my eye level. Still in a sleep state, I wondered if I was dreaming or if it was really happening. I was going to close my sleepy eyes and go back to sleep because I thought I was dreaming. I also thought

I better just check it out and opened my eyes. Realizing the spruce boughs were on fire, I was out of my sleeping bag within seconds. My second reaction, which was a good one, was to pick up the burning baking powder can and throw it out the flap of the tent. I picked it up not realizing it was hot, but I still held on and threw it out the tent.

My fingers were burned, but the wax from the can continued to burn the spruce needles by the stove. It wasn't a big fire, but it was beginning to spread on the spruce boughs. A square of aluminum sat in front of the stove to catch sparks. I picked up the aluminum pad and whopped the flames to death. I realized my whopping was fanning the flames. I was able to squeeze myself between the fire and the tent flap opening. I put my hand outside the flap and grabbed handfuls of snow. I had to grab a few more handfuls before the flames went out. I wasn't taking any chances and dowsed the entire area with snow. I waited until the tent was very cool, wary about going to sleep. I didn't sleep well, thinking sparks waited to begin another round of fire fright-night terrors. I certainly thanked God and my Great Spirit for protecting me. Unreasonable risk was a friend of death.

In the morning, I heard Louison at the cabin door, clanging the old, black frying pan. I was very tired from the previous night's experience. I went back to sleep but then heard Louison shooting the .22 rifle and decided to get the day started and went outside the tent.

Louison poked his gun in the snow and pulled the trigger. What was he doing? He poked in different areas in the snow, shooting the rifle. When he reached his hand beneath the snow where he shot, he pulled a ptarmigan from the snow. I asked him how he knew the ptarmigan were under the snow. He said if I looked closely, I would see little puffs of steam coming from the snow. On very cold days, ptarmigan burrow under the snow to keep warm. The steam was the ptarmigan's breath. I looked in the area and saw tiny puffs of steam coming from holes variably spaced, in the snow. I would never have known the ptarmigan were under the snow, except for what I learned from Louison.

Later in the day, I walked for four hours, farther than I have walked since I arrived on the Barren Lands. I came to a small river in a southerly direction from the main camp. The river was not frozen. It was free flowing with a mist coming off it. It was a sight to see on the Barren Lands in November 1975.

I heard a wolf howl far in the distance. It sounded in anguish or pain. It did not sound like a happy wolf howl. I walked and walked and felt like walking all day and forever. When the sun began to set, I realized I should get back to the cabin. It was past dusk when I stopped to stare from a hill, down at the campsite. It looked miniature, and I saw two figures sawing wood. As I neared the wood-saw, I realized the two men were speaking Chipewyan.

It was Eddy Drybones, Louison's nephew. Soon after we entered the cabin, I saw Richard guide his sleigh into the area where the dogs are tied. Richard and Eddy played crib before Richard sewed dog harnesses with twine. He said the dogs are so strong the threads in the harnesses come apart. We all missed the eclipse of the moon.

On November 19, the sky looked as though someone threw pearl and dusty grey-coloured paint at it to form the image of puffy winter clouds. The men were gone.

I dragged sleeping bag and embroidery into the cabin, before stewing caribou shin bones. I bathed, and as I wrote in my diary I heard Richard yell, "Whoa!" He decided to work on his carriole after we ate, rather than go to an outpost camp. We listened to the radio and went to bed.

Richard and Louison continued trapping in November at different outpost camps but at the same intervals. At the end of November, a white-out surprised us by its suddenness, and we were confined to the cabin for three days. The snow swirled in a fury in all directions. We saw nothing from the cabin windows, except snow. Taller objects were barely visible, and smaller objects were consumed by the steady, falling snow.

Mounds of snow lay on the dogs. Anyone looking down on the dogs would have seen little shapes of white nuggets moving occasionally. I watched one dog try to shake the load, but the snow was too heavy and he fell back into a pure white mound.

Being cabin bound allowed us ample time to prepare the fur for auction. It was my task to comb, yes, comb, the fox fur smooth. I combed over 60 white and 40 coloured fox for both men in one month. Richard and Louison trapped over 125 fox as well as other animals. Richard trapped the most animals. Each man trapped two or three red fox, and Louison trapped a blue fox and a cross fox. The blue fox is called "blue fox" but looks silver. It has a unique colour and is considered a rare catch. The blackish grey fur, with scattered red tips, of the cross fox is also considered a good catch for auction delight.

The fox cycle was high, and it was a good year to trap Barren Land fox. Louison was proud of the two wolves and one wolverine he shot and killed. The most fox Richard came back with from the trapline was 12. Louison loved trapping. Fur from the land to an old-timer like Louison was more precious than gold or diamonds. Every animal was skinned and dried on a stretcher: a piece of wood the size of a fox but narrow at the head of the stretcher.

The weather was fine for hopping hummocks, but we didn't see any caribou. I thought of creating a board game called "Hopping Barren Land Hummocks." I have the design and plan for it in my head and will transfer it to paper one day.

There is an old Tso'Tine–Chipewyan saying: "When the caribou move, they move fast. When the caribou disappear, they disappear like ghosts." We had walked the same route earlier in the fall, but I hadn't written about it. The large white tent we set up was unscathed by the elements or by animals.

We dropped our packs, lit a fire in the tent and warmed up before we cut green poles for three and a half hours. We banked the inner and outer edges of the tent with green poles and spruce boughs. The snow will drift against the tent and form snow banks when the snow falls deep and when roaring Barren Land storms invade the location. The snow banks will act as insulation when it's 40° below.

We gathered brush and dry wood into two large piles, one near the entryway of the tent, and the other a short distance from the tent. During the evening in the tent, we thought we heard Brandy walking around the edges of the tent. Richard and I clearly heard footsteps, or something, walking around the tent perimeter. Brave Richard said to me, "Why don't you go and see if Brandy is still tied up?"

"No! You go! You heard that just as clear as I did," I replied. "What if it's an alien and I'm abducted? What if it's a ghost? What if someone is camping around here who doesn't want us here and does something to me?"

"You have a great imagination," Mr. Courageous said. "Just tie him back up if he's loose."

"I didn't say I was going. Get up and go yourself," I said.

Richard had tied Brandy 20 steps from the back of the tent, in the bush. I was more curious than afraid—well, maybe just a little afraid—to go into the night. I knew Richard wasn't going to check Brandy, so I said to him, "Okay. I'm gone, but just remember, if I'm not back in 10 minutes, you'll know I'm not going to be around…for sure…for a long, long time."

He didn't respond, still nonchalantly doing whatever he was doing, because, he wasn't going anywhere. And to make things worse, Mr. Bold and Daring began telling stories about big hairy hands coming through the tent walls and how the Chipewyan believed the boogeyman still walked the land. I looked at him, wondering if I should go out into the dark but starry night, because a friend from Snowdrift had told me a story about the boogeyman. As a young girl, she was camping with her parents not far from Snowdrift on the edge of the Barren Lands, and she went into the bush to go to the bathroom. She saw a big, hairy man staring at her and rushed back to her parents. No one was around, though, when her father checked the area, but she still swears today she saw what she saw.

The stories told to me were not legends or myths but firsthand experiences worth believing. I lifted the tent flap and went outside. The sky was brilliant with millions of stars. I walked toward Brandy. Along the way, in true scary-movie fashion, an old, dry bush tugged at my hair, and I thought someone was pulling it. I freaked for a moment. Of course, I thought someone or something touched my shoulder, but it was only a tree branch.

I expected Brandy to run to me. "Brandy, you turkey, you better be tied up," I said, approaching a blob of taffy-coloured fur in the bush. He usually stretched and yawned in casual movement and barked when I went to him. The only sound from him was a slow moan: "Ahhh-oooooo." He lay motionless, still tied by rope to the bush. Chills tickled my neck, as though someone or something was watching me. I tripped through the bush fast, back to the tent. Richard was sleeping.

I think I solved the mystery when I awoke the next morning. It was very bright in the tent because of the sunlight. I saw a small animal I think was a mouse scratching at a corner of the tent, scurrying around trying to nibble the supplies. The sound of scurrying and scratching as I lay in my sleeping blanket sounded louder than when I was sitting up. I concluded it was all about acoustics, and indeed a mouse had walked the perimeter of the tent the night before. However, we hadn't been lying on the ground in our sleeping bags when we heard the sounds.

It's October 17, and we have been on the Barren Lands for two months. We left the southerly camp at 11 o'clock. Brandy was happy his load was lighter because we left supplies at the tent for a future journey.

Brandy is an intelligent dog with human-like qualities. Last year, when Richard left the Barrens for Fort Reliance, he said Brandy and another dog were "fooling around and wouldn't get into the harness, so I left them on the Barrens." In the spring, Richard saw something moving on Pike's Portage. He thought it was two wolves. He went across Great Slave Lake from the cabin to Pike's Portage to go wolf hunting but saw it was Brandy and the other dog he'd left on the Barrens. The two dogs had survived four months on the Barren Lands. Richard said the dogs must have eaten old caribou hides, rotten leftover fish or small animals to survive.

The return trip to the main camp was faster and easier. We hopped rocks and hard hummocks and slipped and slid on dew-laden moss. Fortunately, the Mary Francis River was frozen when we crossed it and saved us two hours of walking. I didn't want to cross it, because the river was pure, black ice. I thought a person was never supposed to walk on black ice, but it held our weight. I thanked my feet and God for escaping a potentially cold dunk in freezing water and for the time we saved walking.

When we arrived at the camp, the cabin was warm, and bread dough was rising in a basin. Louison was not at the cabin. For the second time in one day, I looked skyward to praise the Lord when Richard and I walked to Williams Lake to retrieve a fishnet under the ice and the black ice did not crumble under our weight. Richard cut three holes in the ice to pull up the old net—which will not be retired but will be thrown over trees to catch ptarmigan. One sucker fish and two trout were in the fishnet. Richard and I both shot a ptarmigan. When we walked from Williams Lake over a small esker, the snow did not feel dry as it fell, but rather, was wet and quickly melted when it landed on our face, hands and clothing. Snow on the Barren Lands in October is usually firm, not loose and wet.

During the evening after supper, the snow fell fast in huge, steadily falling drifts. I was tired and went to bed early. I could snuggle cozy warm in my sleeping bag in the addition next to the main cabin room and not have to get up to light a stove for warmth during the night.

The next day began with Richard and Louison determined to harness sleighs and drift off on the newly fallen snow. Fifteen dogs stirred quite a commotion, yelping, barking, jumping chains and dancing in all directions to be freed of collar and chain and eager to be harnessed to run. Richard used eight dogs, Louison seven and Siskadoses accounted for the sixteenth dog. It was a repetitious feat to haul one dog at a time from the tie-post and to rope the dog's harness in the sleigh line. The leader was placed last, at the front of the dog line.

When the driver of the sleigh said, "A-Cha!" man and beast were off to the Barren Lands. The dogs were so strong when pulling the sleigh, supplies and master, we had to use a boat anchor to either slow or stop the sleigh. We pulled the anchor when the team was ready to go and dropped it in the snow when we were ready to stop the team.

I plucked ptarmigan, stirred pudding, rolled dough for tarts, peeled vegetables and made stuffing for the ptarmigan. I also made little cheese things in pastry dough. I cooked the tarts all afternoon on the lid of the wood stove. It took a full day to cook on the barrel stovetop.

The men came back and unharnessed the dogs before working on a new stove. One hole was cut in an old, rusted, cherry-red fuel drum for the stovepipes. A second hole was cut at the bottom of the

Dog harnesses in front of the carriole (sleigh) at the dog circle

barrel for the damper. A lid for the damper, cut round from a piece of old tin lying around the entryway room, was screwed on afterwards. The tin looked like a round cookie cutter. The men cut off the bottom quarter of the oil drum. The drum looked dwarfed, at about three feet high.

Although the bottom of the barrel was made of heavy metal, another piece of metal from the previous oil drum stove was placed on the inner bottom. The double layer of metal protected the bottom of the oil drum from the heat of the stove and from burning a hole in the cabin floor. The new stove was lower than the old stove but rounder in diameter. I was happy there was more room to cook on top of the new oil-drum stove.

I placed three tin foil packages filled with ptarmigan and vegetables on the hot coals in the wood stove. It took a half an hour for the birds and vegetables to cook. The "Ptarmigan A-La-La-La-La Barren Lands" tasted great. After washing the supper dishes, I brought pails of fresh, cold drinking water to the cabin and also filled the wood box. I wrote in my diary and went to sleep.

## 🦌 October 19, 1977–October 25, 1977 🦌

OCTOBER 19 WAS A VERY INTERESTING DAY AND PROVED to me there was a spiritual presence on the land. It was an unbelievable experience.

After finishing chores, Richard and I walked in a southeasterly direction and eventually turned straight east. We went farther onto the Barren Lands and scouted for caribou but saw none. The landscape was different from Williams, Tyrrell or the southerly Whitefish or Lynx lakes. Trees were sparse, and there were many small ponds, and bush grew haphazardly. There were no eskers or small hills, and the grey rock was layered with frozen lichen amid wisps of snow. The area had less snow than at Williams Lake. We walked and walked until we saw what looked like a long, well-used and well-worn road.

The pathway was hard-packed with frozen grooves a vehicle passing on it might make. As we walked over a knoll, we saw three caribou slowly walking on what I thought was a man-made road. It was not a road but a caribou path packed hard by millions of caribou over many generations. Animals, and not humans, had made the path, which amazed me. How many generations knew instinctively, or were taught, to take the path of ancestors? What sound, smell, gesture or landscape was embedded in caribou brains to know the path of ancestral caribou from generation to generation? The fragility of caribou could be compared to Aboriginal people's trials and tribulations for survival as Barren Land subsistence hunters and gatherers. Would the caribou, or Aboriginal people, live longer, one generation after another? Would Aboriginal people have caribou to hunt 100 years from now?

What surprised me as we approached the caribou was how the animals did not scatter or run. They looked back at us but slowly turned in the opposite direction and walked away. The caribou we followed walked the long, winding path. It went on for miles, stretching far into the horizon. As we neared the caribou, we noted two very interesting events.

First, we guessed the caribou walking ahead of us were very old, as seen by the length and whiteness of the fur falling like long white beards from under the chin and hanging past the chest. The white beards wavered slightly in the light breeze.

Richard said he was not going to shoot the caribou. I learned years later the caribou we saw were considered by Aboriginal people to be Spirit Caribou. I was glad Richard did not shoot the Elder Spirit Caribou. We didn't need the meat. It would be a shame to kill Elder Spirit Caribou when the walk might be its last, long walk before meeting distant ancestors somewhere down the caribou trail.

The second incident occurred after we crossed the knoll and began to catch up to the Elder Spirit Caribou. The caribou were not only large and tall but also walked at a fast, steady and natural pace. We ran but couldn't keep up.

When we first saw the three caribou, we noticed one animal standing over a lump on the ground. As we neared the lump, we realized it was a fourth caribou trying to rise from the ground. White foam frothed from its mouth, and it had tired, sickly eyes and looked at intervals as though it was going to gag. One of the caribou stood by the sick caribou and wouldn't move as the other two caribou slowly walked down the trail, occasionally stopping to look back at us, and then continued down the caribou trail. It was as though the Elder Spirit Caribou was leaving us to care for the sick caribou. "Maybe the Elder Spirit Caribou thinks we have more powerful medicine. How untrue," I thought.

The caribou on the ground tried to stand, but we saw it had a broken hip and leg. It may have lain on the ground for days without food or water and was slowly dying from its injury. A large herd migrating must have recently passed on the caribou trail, and as in any migration, there were the sick and lame. The caribou on the ground made no sound.

The Elder Spirit Caribou was still in sight, but when Richard and I turned to talk to one another, and then looked down the trail, the Elder Spirit Caribou was gone. We looked farther down the caribou trail, searching in all directions, but did not see any caribou. The trail wound far into the distance and carved a dark path into the Barren Lands. The caribou trail was a sight to see against the backdrop of an azure sky, the edges of which were mixed with dark and light blue and purple, with white wisps of cloud.

I asked Richard what he thought had happened to the lame caribou. He said hundreds of caribou must have passed on the caribou trail onto new migration trails two or three days earlier. He said, when hundreds of caribou are moving fast, "something is bound to happen to some of them." His guess was the caribou had stumbled into a hole or crevasse on the trail and somewhere, somehow, had broken its hip and leg.

I walked around it and saw it try to raise itself, but I also saw the hip bone stick out of the hip socket and the twisted leg. The sick caribou was never going to dance again. The main herd had left, and it was going to die.

I commented to Richard how amazing the Elder Spirit Caribou and younger caribou— the Helper Caribou—were, to remain with the sick caribou until whatever was going to happen to it happened. Richard said he was going to shoot it to put it out of its misery, and we could pack the meat back to camp. I told him if he was going to shoot it, we certainly weren't going to eat it.

"Look at its eyes, Richard. It's sick. Look at the white stuff coming out of its mouth. You want to eat it, you can eat it, not me. You want to carry the carcass back to camp, go ahead, not me! We shouldn't even touch it! What if it's carrying some kind of caribou disease humans die from? We don't know what is really wrong with it. Let's just leave it here. I don't want to die at the Barren Land camp like John Hornby just because you wanted to bring some sick caribou back."

Richard looked concerned as he watched the struggling caribou and agreed with me. He shot the sick caribou. It didn't have much energy or life in it, because it didn't flinch and died instantly. I said wolves or another animal would feed on its carcass if the black flies didn't pick it to its bones first. Richard agreed, and we didn't touch it. We left the dead caribou on the Barren Lands.

We walked the caribou trail until dusk and didn't see another caribou, so turned off the caribou path in the direction of the cabin. When we reached the cabin, we told the story to Louison, who at first said he was worried about where we were. Louison said Richard's assessment of the caribou was correct. Sometimes, he said, fast-moving caribou are skittish. Some caribou fall down, some get tripped up in holes or some are simply bumped while running and get trampled. Louison agreed with me about not taking the meat. He said any caribou injured by an accident caused by the herd is not a good caribou to eat and is considered bad luck to take.

I cooked caribou in gravy with paste-board potato glue and cream corn. After we ate our meal, I thought about the caribou on the Barrens. There was nothing we could do for it even if we were caribou doctors. It would have died the way it was meant to die. No caribou on the land would have stayed to feed it, to give it water, to put its hip back into its socket or to fix a broken leg, and neither could we. I found it interesting the Elder Spirit Caribou and the Helper Caribou had stayed by the sick caribou's side until humans came to ensure its final hour.

On October 20, the three of us left the main camp. It was a bright, sunny day to travel. Louison was going to a second southerly outpost camp, and Richard and I planned to travel to the seven-mile camp also in a southerly direction from the main camp. The time it would take to get to the camp depended on whether the dogs veered from the main trail.

Before we left, Louison showed us old hunting and trapping camps when we walked with him before we parted ways on the trail. He showed us the areas where the people from Tso'Tine of Rocher River, Métis from Yellowknife and Akaitcho and Dogrib from Fort Rae camped. He said Aboriginal people from Snowdrift and Fort Resolution used to trap, and still trapped, in the area, "sometimes, but not like before."

En route to the camp was the first time I travelled in the carriole, bundled and bouncing across the land. Five dogs pulled the sleigh and two passengers. Richard wanted to train a new dog, Turk, as a leader, to have two leaders. Turk didn't respond well to Richard's commands to go left or right, resulting in a three-hour delay arriving at the camp. The dogs were tired. I jumped out of the sleigh and coaxed Turk up a very steep hill before the sleigh glided to the front of the tent.

The tent was intact and hadn't been destroyed by curious animals. In the tent, I arranged supplies and sleeping bags. I tied items in canvas bags to the ridgepole of the tent to prevent any access from animals and to avoid thawed snow damage to container contents. Richard stayed outdoors to set traps in mounds of snow, because he said he saw a fox run over a nearby hill. He said it was a good sign for the time of year. He set a shaved green pole in the middle of hard-packed mounds of snow and attached a chain to the pole. He opened the claws of the trap and baited it with smelly, frozen fish before sprinkling the trap and bait with snow to hide it from animals. When it snowed, the green pole above the snow showed the trap's location. When an animal stepped onto the snow-covered pan of the trap, the claws shut fast to hold its foot or leg.

I picked and plucked dry wood from dead trees for evening and morning fires. Tyke, one of the dogs, barked loudly in a silent, late afternoon.

As I sawed a log, I heard Richard in the distance, crunching snow as he walked. It was past dusk when I opened the tent flap to see the land covered with a ghostly mist. I could not see the tent two feet in front of me when I carried extra brush and wood inside the tent.

I remembered the dogs had barked steadily the past few nights at Williams Lake. We thought it was a wolf or fox wandering around the fish stage down by the shoreline. Richard set three traps around the fish stage, saying he didn't think an animal would come close to it. When he checked the traps the following day, a cross fox was in one of the traps. It was Richard's first trapped animal of the season.

I cooked fish, and we ate drymeat and drank tea at the seven-mile outpost camp. I sewed moccasins, and Richard sewed dog harnesses. He wanted two dogs running in tandem, or two dogs running in a straight line ahead, with the other dogs behind the two front dogs running in a fanned out V-formation. Bill Carpenter of Bowspringer Kennels in Yellowknife had given Richard the idea to run the dogs in tandem. He also gave Richard two dogs to run to see how the dogs would perform on the Barren Lands because he was breeding dogs to try to bring back the original strain of the northern husky.

The next day, the weather was bleak. It was as foggy as it was the night before. Richard said colder weather was coming and we should leave the camp. We were going to travel to the main camp in a semicircle on the land, but because we were headed in the direction of Tyrrell Lake, he said we should check the camp and set traps on the way. The sleigh crunched over snow and ice.

Some of the dogs performed well in harness and some dogs did not perform as well as Richard hoped. Sitting in the sleigh, I could see four little legs running, running, running, and then one dog would decide it was tired, and it would slow down. A second dog running next to the slow runner continued to keep the pace, leaving the slow runner behind, so the whole line became tangled.

I made a second observation while sitting in the sleigh, and the first time I saw it, I didn't believe what I saw. The dogs ran an even pace, and all of a sudden, one would do a squat-run, emptying its last meal. It was amazing to me how a dog could squat, shit and run at the same time without bumping its bum on the ground, still in harness and without disrupting the other dogs. It had to be a learned habit. The seasoned dogs knew how to complete the rhythmic feat, whereas newer dogs stopped the whole team to leave droppings on the trail.

From the sleigh, it was a merry-go-round of activity watching the dogs. One dog would travel on, keeping pace, and a second dog would suddenly stop. The first dog wasn't expecting the second dog to stop and was yanked by the neck and dragged on, or it waited until the first dog dropped his load. The doggy bathroom stop tangled the whole team. It was the Barren Land Dog Shat Waltz in musical league: one stoop, poop, dog drop, stop, all dogs get tangled in the harness, Richard swears and untangles the dogs, the dogs begin to pull and the whole process begins again. The dogs pulled fast again when the whip was cracked. One dog actually looked back at Richard to see if he was watching him, and I wondered what the dog was thinking. The dog then kept running, eyes straight ahead as though he understood Richard's stern look "to keep on truckin'."

Richard often ran ahead of the dog team. I seldom did, but sometimes I ran beside the sleigh. It was my station in life to sit in the sleigh. I thought we were travelling to Tyrrell Lake, but somewhere in the distance I smelled smoke. At two o'clock we were riding the twisted trail to the cabin. Richard tied the tired dogs when we arrived.

I cooked supper, and Richard fed the dogs. I was exhausted, though I didn't think I did anything to account for my fatigue.

On October 22, we travelled to Tyrrell Lake to set a fishnet under the ice. What a trip!

Brandy, the old leader, was at the helm, and disaster reigned from the moment the words, "GO, you little bastard!" were hollered. Brandy would not move. He just stood still at the head of the dog team. When Richard cracked the whip, we were off like a bolt of lightning. Brandy, on the trail, just meandered his way slowly until Richard took him out of lead and put another dog, Michael, in lead.

We finally reached a lake we named "No Name Lake" and took the poles, fishnet, sinkers and sinker line, rocks and buoys out of the sleigh and carried the items to the middle of the lake. Richard chopped 18 holes in the ice and pushed a pole attached to a long line under the ice from hole to hole until the line reached the last of the 18 holes. The ice was soft because there was a south wind, and it was warm on the Barren Lands. Whoever was at the 18th hole pulled the long line until the fishnet was seen. Richard was at the first hole nearest the shoreline, and I was at the 18th ice hole, farther out on the black ice. The end of the fishnet was in sight, and it began to rain. It actually rained on the Barren Lands on October 22 where we stood on the frozen lake, setting a fishnet under the ice.

I was scared to walk around the 18th hole for fear the ice was going to break. The slush was thick, and I thought for sure the ice was going to crack under my weight. Richard appeased me by measuring the depth of the lake at the 18th fish hole. He tied a rock to a rope and dropped it into the dark watery hole. He said it measured 60 feet deep. It made me even more fearful knowing the depth of the lake, and I decided to unravel another fishnet at the shoreline because I didn't want to lose my life over a fishnet.

When we first set the net, the rope holding it broke, and I had to hold tight to the net so it wouldn't slip forever under the ice. I thought I would stand on it to hold it down but realized it was a bad idea when one of my feet became tangled in it. The net's weight didn't pull me into the watery hole. I was quick to untangle my moccasins and step away from the potential danger of being dragged by the heavy, wet fishnet.

We had to set the net again, and our second attempt was successful, which made Richard happy. Instead of going on to Tyrrell Lake, we decided to go back to the main camp. The fishnet at No Name Lake was set about a mile from the Tyrrell Lake camp. We should have gone to the Tyrrell Lake outpost camp.

It was an adventure trying to get to the main cabin in the rain. We saw a cross fox run over a hill. The rain sloshed away clear paths of snow to reveal the natural environment of rock, bush and moss. It was like running dogs through muskeg. It was a hard pull for the dogs. I did my share of exercise, running to keep in sight of the sleigh. As we neared the cabin, I saw the sunset. It was red, red, red, all the way down the line. The evening was incredibly warm and beautiful.

I fed the dogs and stood for the longest time to feel the warm air and see the sunset dance a slow, slip and fade behind the Barren Land night clouds in the west.

During supper, Louison said when he left the cabin for his outpost camp, he was crossing Williams Lake near Gus D'Aoust's old trapping grounds when he broke through the ice with the dogs and carri- ole. He said two of the dogs near the back of the sleigh were in the lake, with half the sleigh sub- merged, and he was up to his waist in water. It was fortunate he was near the shoreline, or we would have wondered all winter where he disappeared. "Yeah, me just about die. Me just about go to hell. That's okay. Me make good firewood down there!"

The weather was mild, but I don't think the men liked the melting snow. Richard scouted for caribou on October 23. Later in the day, Richard and Louison decided to build a new sleigh, retrieving the plywood bent earlier in the fall. When untying the rope and pulling the nails from the tree stump, the men had to be careful, because the pressure from the boards, once released, would have slapped the person with great force.

After supper, I dug up one of the fish holes we had plugged with moss. Let me tell you, the smell from the fish hole was the most rank I ever allowed my nose to smell. There was no doubt about it: the fish were absolutely rotten. Richard said the stinkies were in better shape than the fish he and Louison had packed last year. By "better shape," I assumed Richard meant the smell was worse than the previous year.

It was quite a chore pulling frozen moss off the top of the hole, fighting to separate the dead smellies and scraping moss and sand off the frozen fish with a wooden scraper. It was a difficult task when wearing bright yellow, slippery plastic gloves to slice the half-frozen, slimy, slithery tails and then hang the fish on poles on the fish stage. The fish were so rotten some of the fish-tails just fell off the fish. Once the job was completed, I knew any red, white, cross, blue or silver fox, or every wolf and cinnamon grizzly bear or wolverine, would have loved to come right up to me and eat me. I smelled as smelly as the smelliest smell you could smell.

Richard caught a rabbit in a trap by the fish stage and skinned it. He had to kill it first, though, because it was still alive in the trap.

Later on, Richard opened a bottle of whiskey, and we all sipped it. We were all on our best behaviour, meaning we controlled our consumption.

It was a lazy day on October 24. Snow and ice crystals beat on the window plastic all night long. I walked to check two traps on nearby hills but not one animal had taken the bait.

Everything was covered with ice. Every willow, leaf, tree, rock, hard-packed frozen footprint— everything in sight was iced. The outdoor toilet door wouldn't open because of the ice. Later in the afternoon when I photographed the ice on the meat-cutting table and meat-drying rack, I felt the effects of the ice storm. I thought it was rain. It wasn't rain but tiny ice pins, which immediately froze upon hitting any object.

Pepper in the wind: it reminded me of pepper in the wind. I couldn't believe how fast the weather changed. One minute it's a grey, drabby, miserable winter's day, and the next minute, I was in a pepper-ice storm, stinging me as I hid my camera close to my chest and covered my head with my

An ice storm covered the carriole Richard and Louison were building, the meat-drying rack, bush and everything in sight.

parka hood. My hands felt the sting of each burst of cutting ice as I snapped the camera shutter.

"Ow, ow," I kept saying, but still snapped pictures. I only shot a few frames before running into the cabin to regroup.

"Do you know that rain is not rain," I said to Louison and Richard. "It's like rain before it hits you, then when it hits you, it turns to small pieces of ice. This is the strangest thing I've ever seen." I put on gloves, covered my head and face entirely because I did not want to feel a thousand, tiny, constantly darting knives hit my bare skin.

"Yeah. Oh, sure," was the uninterested response.

Well, for me it was a revelation, and I wanted to be a part of it—sting or no sting on the flesh. I am happy to report some of the photographs turned out well but didn't truly represent what it felt like. No one will know the effect of the white pepper on my welted, red hands. Each place where the ice hit me were little welts, reminding me of red chicken pox. The pin-pain didn't last long and neither did the little red welts. It was the immediacy of the occasion keeping the memory alive. It was all quite interesting. I had never before seen ice pins rain down from the sky.

I quickly took some pictures and ran back to the cabin. Louison and Richard made comments about never seeing the weather so strange. I sat in a corner on one of the beds most of the afternoon because Louison and Richard brought Louison's sleigh into the cabin to thaw, and it filled the main living space. Soon, I would have to wash clothes because the pile was growing. Richard came back from a walk with seven ptarmigan. After supper, I cleaned the ptarmigan and put the defeathered and cleaned birds in a basin of cold water in the outer room: our "refrigerator." The cold water rid the birds of excess blood.

I went to bed early because I felt ill. Richard gave me prescription drugs, which I enjoyed while in and out of sleep. He brought a small canvas pouch with various prescription drugs. I don't think we used the drugs more than three times during the months we were on the land.

The next day, with rest and pills, I felt fine. Louison left the main camp for his "first tent," five miles from the main campsite. Richard and I went to the southerly seven-mile camp by dog team. The dogs were difficult to harness. One dog, Brutus, fought with one of the red dog twins and wouldn't release the dog. Brutus was the strongest dog I have ever seen. One time he pulled the loaded sleigh and resting dogs, plus me and Richard, by himself, because all he wanted to do was to work and pull the sleigh. Richard beat Brutus with a rope but he wouldn't release his stronghold on the red dog. Finally Richard cracked the whip, and all the dogs scattered. Three of the dogs were bloodied from fighting. Richard asked me to crack the whip while he reharnessed the dogs, and then we were off to Tyrrell Lake.

Brutus was frothing at the mouth as we reached Tyrrell Lake so we put him in the sleigh for a while and then let him run the last 100 yards to the campsite. When I asked Richard why the dog would froth at the mouth, he said the only reason he could think of was because Brutus had overexerted himself in the harness. He said the dog was overtired, but he was fine once fed and tied to a dog post.

Earlier in the fall, Richard had dug a square area in the dirt and sand. He banked the perimeter of the area with logs and then set a white tent in position on the dirt floor with the tent edges curled around the logs. An old worn tent was thrown over the new tent and tied to it. One log acted as the ridgepole set in the middle of the inside of the tent.

The tent was built to step down onto the dirt floor on entry. He also constructed a rectangular door made from green poles and nailed caribou hides over the poles. Hinges on the sides of the poles allowed the caribou-skin door to swing open and close. The stovepipe on the BC Heater stove was too small to allow smoke to escape out of it quickly, so inside, the tent filled with smoke. Richard opened the tent flap to rid the tent of smoke. I walked outside while the smoke was filtering out of the tent.

We sawed wood and picked brush for the morning fire. The brush was hung upside down on the ridgepole near the stove to dry. It dried quickly in the warm tent and was ready for the morning fires. Richard boiled traps to rid the claws of the smell of animals previously caught with the traps. We pulled sticks to see who would sleep on the green-pole bed. It was too spindly on my back; if I had won, I would have forfeited the win. I slept on the dirt and spruce bough floor. It was comfortable in my sleeping bag, but melted water from the top of the stovepipe dripped on my face most of the night. I moved halfway under the bed Richard lay on and

The outpost camp at Tyrrell Lake, about five to seven miles from the main campsite, with a caribou-skin door and frozen trout leaning against the tent

then returned to my original spot and didn't get a good night's sleep. I only slept when I snuggled almost to the bottom of my sleeping bag.

## 🦌 October 26, 1977–November 1, 1977 🦌

ON OCTOBER 26, RICHARD AND I SET A SECOND NET ON Tyrrell Lake using the same method we had used to set the first net. The weather was foggy.

One minute we couldn't see the tent on the hill because of the fog, and the next moment the land was clear. I had to look down at the ice with every step I took when walking backwards to set the net. I didn't want to step with my mukluks on the overflow; otherwise, my mukluks and five pairs of socks would have been soaked.

The fishnet was heavy for me to hold. I slowly allowed it to filter through my fingers, and, at the same time, held the net so it wouldn't be pulled too fast into the ice hole. We succeeded in setting the net. The evening seemed very bright, even though it was overcast.

Early the next morning, we packed the sleigh and harnessed the dogs. It was difficult to set traps. The toe line loosened from the sleigh, and Richard had to pull it while standing at the back of the sleigh. He cut his hand badly. We checked the nets on Tyrrell Lake, and one fish was quite large.

We finally arrived at the main campsite, after winding past the curve in the hill on the trail and bending through willows. We could smell the wood smoke and see it rise from the stovepipe.

"If Louison's home," Richard said, "I wonder why the dogs aren't barking." There was an ominous, quiet feeling in the air. Something was not right with the world at Williams Lake.

which was not agreeable to my taste buds or my stomach. No wonder some people call homemade brew "rotgut."

Richard came back with three ptarmigan and sipped brew with us until I made supper. I went to bed around 10 o'clock, but Richard and Louison stayed up talking about trapping.

On November 20, I completed chores: I washed dishes, swept the cabin floor, chipped ice and filled the water pail, filled the wood box, brought brush into the outer cabin, brought supplies from the food stage and emptied the slop pail. I scraped a bull hide while Richard and Louison walked to find ptarmigan. I cooked three ptarmigan in a stew. Amazingly, we have plenty of onions, but the carrots, turnips and potatoes are gone. The onions and turnips lasted the longest without rotting in the root cellar.

We all played poker at night, but the men gave up because I won almost every hand. I returned to scraping the hide. It was easier than the first time I scraped a hide. Louison suggested I hang it over a pole on the drying rack above the stove. Richard helped me scrape the hide, and it turned a soft, creamy colour and was velvety when touched.

We all packed to travel by dogs on November 21. Louison said he wanted to go to the Hanbury River outpost camp and would bring back some musk oxen. He said, "Government mens don't know one musk ox missing anyway." He didn't bring back musk oxen meat though.

We were on the trapline by 10:00 AM. Today is the coldest day I have ever experienced since being on the Barren Lands. I was cold before I hopped onto the sleigh. My feet, hands and nose tip got the worst of the cold. My intuition said, "Stay home. You are going to regret this day."

There was one white fox in a trap near the Tyrrell Lake tent. My body felt frozen. A cold west wind blew. I would rather have clear and cold than windy and cold. My fingers were so cold I had to warm my hands inside my parka and couldn't strike a match to light the stove. I finally lit the paper and wood, and the stove roared. I warmed my hands and fingers. Louison said to knead my knees, feet, hands or any other body part when it became too cold. We ate between three o'clock and four o'clock. It was so dark outside, it looked like midnight.

Richard came back with a white fox and skinned it, making sure he cleaned the death scene before we ate. He fed the dogs. It was cold outside, and mega heat escaped when the tent door was opened; the tent cools fast when the door is opened. The dogs became excited around seven o'clock. Richard said it was either a visitor, which was rare, or a fox caught in a trap. He returned from the darkness with a hoar-frosted white fox and said it was worth a $50–$75 walk in the cold, night air. Two fox caught in the same trap on the same day "must be good luck" he said.

On November 22, Richard and I finally decided to travel to the farthest outpost campsite. He wanted to set a net and tent in the same area. For the next two hours, all I saw were my beaver mitts, ice and snow. The northwest wind was so cold I couldn't think of adjectives to accurately describe it. We arrived at a point in the land where Richard said the Mary Francis River flows out of Tyrrell Lake and into the Thelon River. When we arrived at our destination, I thought I would freeze to death; I was so cold. I wore three pairs of wool mittens and one pair of beaver mitts and my hands were still frozen.

Richard walked to a nearby hill to cut green poles for tent poles, to check for caribou tracks and to see what the Mary Francis River looked like when frozen steam rose on open water at −100°F. The dogs howled and danced from foot to foot because of the cold and wanted to move.

It was the worst time to have to go to the bathroom. I unzipped my coats, and instant cold hit my body. I pulled all pairs of pants down and squatted to go to the bathroom. I had to wipe. In the time it took to take my hand out of my parka, wipe and bring my hand back to my parka, it was frozen. In seconds, my bottom would freeze too. "To hell with wiping," I said and tried to pull up my multilayered pairs of pants.

I barely pulled all pants to my waist when I realized my hands wouldn't operate. I was so frustrated at not being able to fully pull up my pants, zip my coat and warm my hands—I just stood still allowing the wind to whip me. I began to cry, wishing I had never come to the Barren Lands, literally freezing my ass off. I have never been so cold in my life. I repeatedly called Richard to come and help me, and when he did come to help, he asked, "What's the matter? Are you cold?"

I was so angry, I screamed, "What the fuck do you mean am I cold?! I can't do my pants up, I can't zipper my coat, my hands won't move. I'm chilled to the bone, my feet are frozen and you ask me if I'm cold?! I promise you this—I am never, NEVER, going to live on the Barren Lands again! And you're so stupid to bring us out here when it's probably 100 degrees below zero." He let me stand for a moment before he helped me, saying, "More like 70 below with a wind chill."

Richard finally agreed it was too cold a day to travel; we had travelled farther than he wanted to travel, and he said we should head in a "homeward direction." He didn't go back to either Tyrrell Lake or Williams Lake. Instead, he drove the dogs to a grove of trees. He said it was a good spot for a tent. I didn't like the spot. It was a "nothing" spot. There was totally nothing around except piles and mountains of snow with one short, little scraggly tree.

I certainly learned a lesson in history from the experience. There is no way Sir John Franklin and his men could have survived a Barren Land winter in meagre, thin, British clothing. The romantic pictures in history books I have seen showing Franklin's men walking in light clothing, pulling heavy sleighs in storms was fiction, not fact. There is no way any person could have survived the High Arctic, where it is colder and darker for longer periods of time than where we were on the Barren Lands, and walk around in thin, light clothing, as depicted in the history books I studied in school.

I could barely move my hands from the time it took to pull down my pants, squat, wait to go to the bathroom and pull my pants up. I wore layers of clothing and was frozen by the wind and cold, and Franklin's men only wore thin jackets and one thin pair of pants. What did Franklin's men use for toilet paper after walking in the snow for a month?

I will never be convinced Franklin's men survived any length of time once off the ship and walking on land in winter. On the Barren Lands there are small shrubs, but in the High Arctic, there are few shrubs, and, I believe, the winds and cold are worse. Franklin's men would have had to scrape moss for fires, if it wasn't buried under mounds and groves of snow. What did they eat to provide strength and energy needed to survive the High Arctic, presuming the men were alive for months, when the food on the sleighs disappeared?

The stories of Franklin's men surviving the land for long periods of time is a myth, created by eager men wishing for a romantic tragedy they themselves never lived.

Sir George Back (1796–1868) and Warburton Pike (1861–1915), both arctic adventurers, recorded Barren Land trips and drew pictures to prove the journeys were authentic. Back and Pike hired Aboriginal people as guides and reported expeditions in journals. Both men did not seek mythical anticipation to become costly, lifelong legends. In fact, Pike did not favour large, well-financed expeditions. He lived off the land as did the Aboriginal people who travelled with him as his guides. He wrote the well-documented *The Barren Ground of Northern Canada* and kept a journal and sketches in 1889, depicting the land and life of the Barren Lands from Fort Resolution to Coppermine, Aylmer Lake and Lac De Gras. Why create anticipation only to fuel fires of romanticism and the sensibilities of unfounded speculation?

Although Back volunteered and served under Sir John Franklin on three expeditions to the North, he was not on the fatal Franklin Expedition. He instead commanded his own overland expeditions to survey and explore the Great Fish River ("Thlew-ee-choc" in

Chipewyan/Tso'Tine language) systems, which were later named the Back River systems. In 1833, Back lived at Old Fort Reliance, where three chimneys still stand in the dwellings the Back party lived in during the winter.

I believe Franklin's men died from disease and mental and physical anguish, which has been recorded, and the men's remains were eaten by animals or by each other. I think most of the men froze. No Inuit have recorded and authenticated meeting Franklin's men, though newer generations recall ancestors' stories about meeting and helping Franklin or his men.

Which stories are legends and which are myth? Which are true and which are untrue? I am not a Franklin buff, but after the cold I experienced today, I will never believe either Franklin or his men survived when harsh winter set in on the land. My opinion, analysis and assessment would be true for any explorer or adventurer unprepared for the Barren Lands.

I was warmer once the sleigh was unloaded and the wood was cut. A huge snow pile was shovelled aside so we could set up the tent. Richard said we would sleep one night in the tent and leave for Williams Lake the next day.

We were on the fringes of a cold land where we could see nothing for miles except blowing snow on acres of snow-bound terrain. In the tent, I arranged gear and lit the fire in the frozen stove. I boiled tea while Richard fed the dogs and set traps near the tent. The wind blew stronger. I slept in two sleeping bags and was still cold despite being fully clothed.

## 🦌 November 23, 1977—November 29, 1977 🦌

ONE MORE DAY ON THE FROZEN BARREN LANDS. IT WAS too windy and snowy to go anywhere. Boredom was ever-present. I gathered brush where I could dig it from under the snow and broke branches from the only scraggly tree in sight. A cold, frozen ice mist over the land impaired visibility. A great ring of bland bluish-brown, lemonade-yellow colour revolved around the sun, signalling a storm. The stormy weather encased the land and blew the carriole over.

During early afternoon, I was going to fry fish, but the lard was frozen hard. I did a foolish thing. I used a large knife to break the lard piece by piece. My left hand held the lard, and I used my right hand to stab at the rock-hard lard. My left thumb was in the wrong place at the wrong time. I wiggled the knife, putting weight on the middle part of the lard, and the knife slipped and... slice. The knife slipped in the lard and sliced my left thumb. I felt the knife cut into my flesh and felt the pain.

The sudden cut made me light-headed and nauseous as I watched blood pour out in spurts. I repeated to myself in shock: "What should I do? What should I do? What should I do? Should I put it outside in the cold snow?" I placed my thumb in the snow. It stung badly, and the bleeding didn't stop. Realizing the blood wasn't clotting, Richard said to raise my arm above my head.

He tore toilet paper and ripped off a piece of his shirt to act as a bandage and wrapped the wound tight. I turned white and told Richard I was going to faint. "Don't faint," he said. "Lie down." The cut continued to bleed but slowly ceased. It ached and throbbed all night. I thought sticking my hand out the tent flap would allow the cold to sooth the cut, but instead, it hurt more with the cold on it.

I coddled my hand in the warmth of my sleeping bag, thinking, "Oh, no! I'm going to bleed to death in a small tent I didn't want to be in, in the first place, in the middle of Sam's Land (Sam McGee), and then what will Richard do with my body? Will he cremate me like Sam McGee?" It wasn't my time to meet Sam.

Tent life went on, despite temperatures I guessed would be, oh, say, –1000°F with a wind chill of –2000°F! I washed dishes as I sat on my sleeping blanket, with limited finger movement. Richard checked nearby traps and came back with a white fox. Tyke got loose during the night and ate the fish we brought.

Richard said he had enough of the adventure, and if the weather was nice tomorrow, we would travel to the Tyrrell Lake camp. He skinned the fox. I didn't feel well and lay down to rest.

On the morning of November 24, the sleigh was packed to travel. It was still very cold, but the wind did not blow wildly, and the sunrise showed signs of a sunny, blue-sky day.

The dogs were excited to move after lying in white snow mounds for two days. I sure thanked God when wood logs were put over the tent flap and the walls were banked with snow. I was so happy to be bumping along in the sleigh away from "the frozen place of hell's creation." I was very happy Richard decided not to camp at Tyrrell Lake. He was happy to collect 12 white fox en route to Williams Lake.

The dogs did not eat for two days and were fed fish at the Tyrrell Lake camp. The dogs chewed and gulped the rotten smelly dead fish. Thank God we were finally back at the main camp. My "station in life" was to light the lantern, light the stove, unpack the carriole and haul items into the cabin. I cleaned my thumb with peroxide and warm water. I didn't realize the depth and length of the cut. I smoothed ointment over the cut and bandaged it using the items I found in the first aid kit. It was not infected but was still very painful.

I cooked supper as the dogs howled a welcome for Louison. He looked at my thumb and said, "Next time, cut hard things lay down. Don't hold and cut. One time, I trapped at Timber Bay. Me and a friend trapped at Timber Bay. Me and my friend were checking nets. He took the ice pick and put it in the sleigh. The ice pick stood straight at the front. Just like that." Louison demonstrated how the ice pick stood vertical. He continued, "The ice pick stood at the front of the sleigh. My friend was trying to stop the dogs and sleigh.

"The ice pick flew up and hit my friend in the leg, and it went right through his leg." Louison indicated where on his leg the ice pick had gone through his friend's leg.

"Hey, hey, hey, the sleigh, just full of blood. It was like my friend was just dead. I blew on my friend's leg to stop the bleeding. The bleeding stopped. We travelled all the way to Snowdrift by dog team. My friend went by plane to Yellowknife. The doctor cut the leg off...took it right off."

Boiling water to wash dishes, I thought about what Louison said when he said, "I blew on my friend's leg to stop the bleeding." I heard medicine men could blow on people's wounds or any part of the body to heal people. I just accepted it was what he did to help his friend. I also couldn't dismiss the time earlier in the fall when I saw Louison carrying a huge rock from a distance. He walked with the rock on his back, then plunked it down by the main outer porch door. I didn't believe it was as heavy as it was until I tried to lift it. I couldn't budge it. It was then I thought of him as a medicine man because there was no way anyone his age should have been able to carry such a heavy rock even three feet. He carried it from somewhere on the Barren Lands and said he wanted it to pound drymeat.

I washed dishes with one hand, and Richard and Louison dried the dishes. Richard kept taking the dishes to dry. Louison said, "I wait a long time for nothing." He hung the dish towel to dry and laughed. The men drank brew and skinned fox and told Barren Land stories. Louison said he stopped by one of Richard's traps and brought him one more white fox.

On November 25, Richard dug the remaining fish from the stinky hillside. We were indecisive about whether to travel to an outpost camp.

Louison cut wood and hunted ptarmigan. As I was washing dishes, Louison came to the cabin with a white fox caught on the other side of the drinking-water lake. It was in one of my traps. I was excited and decided to set two more traps. I set the traps in a direction I thought the fox would run. The sky looked threatening, with a big black cloud hanging over Williams Lake. I returned to the cabin and cleaned the cabin and washed clothes.

Louison and Richard cut more wood. I only washed the towels and white clothing. I couldn't wring water from the clothes well because of my injured thumb.

Later in the evening, Louison cut a pattern for a caribou-hide coat. Richard lined his caribou-skin sleeping bag with duffle and joked about making "a great big caribou-skin sleeping bag for both of us to sleep in."

There is one more month to the day until it is Christmas Day.

On November 26, Richard and I travelled to the southerly outpost camp. It was a most beautiful day and a good day to travel. The dogs pulled the sleigh well. I sat in the sleigh watching the frozen snow-covered land pass by at about five miles per hour, but it wasn't a cold ride. Richard was happy because he trapped three fox, but my traps were empty.

We packed spruce boughs and snow around the tent. Richard said the tent seeped heat fast because it was too big. The stove was stuffed with green wood and we let it burn all night. Richard skinned one fox but left the majority of fox in the sleigh to skin later.

Did I say I would never go to the farthest ends of the unknown Barren Land universe again? I lied. When we passed Tyrrell Lake en route to the small tent, I cringed at the thought of what happened on my last visit: freezing my butt off, cutting my thumb and enduring boredom because we were snowed in for two days. The small tent was snowed in but hadn't been trashed by a grizzly. The first trip was a disaster. The second trip was too brief to notice, and the third trip was interesting, considering the fight I had with a white fox...

The event began in early evening when the dark sky invaded the band of crimson-orange on the horizon. I walked in thigh-deep snow down a slope on the bleak Barren Lands to a trap Richard had set. As I approached it, I saw the white fox, its forepaw partially caught, frantically attempting to pull it from the trap. I believed I was more afraid of it than it was of me. I was brave when I removed dead fox from traps, but a live fox wiggling and squirming meant I had to do something with it. I looked at it. It looked at me.

"Do what comes naturally," an inner voice said. "Hit it on the nose with the axe and take it out of the trap. Wring its neck when it's stunned and drag it to the tent." It's nice to hear your own thoughts give you advice, but try, upon approach, to grab a small, white, wriggling animal.

When I grabbed at it, it caw-haaaaed, like Sleeping Beauty's evil witch from the big, bad North. I jumped back, looking at it. It wasn't supposed to caw-haaaa at me. It was supposed to stand there and let me do whatever I chose to do with it. We eyed each other, bracing for the next round.

"You're a little shit-head and you don't want to die, do you? But…you're going toooooo," I warned it in a sing-song voice.

The fox looked at me, its dark, oval beady eyes hidden behind pure white fur. I hit it on the nose with the axe but missed its nose and hit it on the cheek. It didn't whine, cry or make a noise. It knew I was the dangerous one and looked at me trying to free its paw from the trap.

I tried to hit it on the nose and succeeded, but it still wasn't stunned. I swung hard, and it fell down, dead, or so I thought. I poked it with the axe, but it didn't move. I cautiously took its paw out of the trap, watched in case it moved and dragged it to one side of the snow. I turned to reset the trap. I was happy knowing I would carry a white fox back to camp.

I turned just in time to see my white fox limp away, staring back at me heading west toward the crimson-orange fading sunset, singing—probably singing—"Happy trails to you, until we meet again…."

Yep! Me big Métis womanz trapper of the North! I picked up the axe and walked to the tent with a fine tale to spin in the warmth of a winter's tent.

On November 28, Richard and I pulled the dogs and sleigh to the top of the steep hill by the small tent, ready to journey to Williams Lake. I was amazed we didn't tip the sleigh racing down the hill. We didn't stop at the Tyrrell Lake camp but continued on to Williams Lake. The dogs ran fast as we rounded the corner in the bush leading to the trail of the inner dog's circle at the main camp.

Turk became a very good leader. He knew his role and led the sleigh in a straight line rather than random. Richard took seven fox from traps. The process of skinning fox in the cabin continued.

There was another interesting occurrence on the Barren Lands on November 29.

From November 29 to December 4, the three of us continued an ordered existence at the main and outpost camps. We checked traps, gathered wood from distant locations during cold days in dull, depressing weather. I had time to sit on my thinking hill to survey the land in peace, bundled in my winter clothing in a clump of deep snow. There have been "strange days" on the Barren Lands, and today, another strange event occurred.

The men gathered wood, and I decided to walk the hill where I sat and thought about life. I had seen the figure of an animal walk the land in the distance and thought it was either a wolf or wolverine. I saw it two years ago. I saw it in the late fall, and today we met.

The snow was deep on my thinking hill. My ritual was to stomp a space in the deep snow, with my hood and scarves pulled tight over my head, and sit in the snow mould. I peered in all directions through the slit in the woollen scarves.

It was a beautiful November day to sit on the Pre-cambrian Shield and watch the dark snow clouds in one great patch across the sky forecast a pending winter storm. There was a light breeze but it wasn't cold. The dogs snuggled and slept under snow blankets, reminiscent of little igloos, and were unaware of nearby activities. I scoured the land, and at one point thought I saw a movement at the top of the hill where the radio antennae wire was attached to a pole on the hill behind Big Bad John.

It was an animal moving at a slow, cautious pace. It walked unhurried down the hillside, past Big Bad

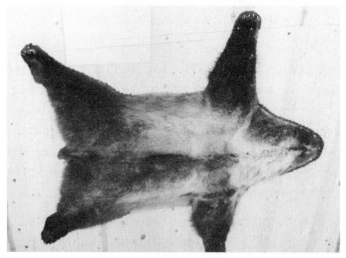

A wolverine skin tacked to plywood

John, to the main cabin door, occasionally sniffing the air and ground. It was a medium- to large-sized wolverine. It was sleek black with a yellow-bronze strip running from its mid-forehead over the head and down the back to its tail tip, and it had white paws. Except for the colouring, it looked like a big skunk with a shorter tail.

I did not move a muscle but watched it wind its way toward the meat-cutting stand. In a few yards, if it kept walking in the same direction, it would dawdle to the bottom of the hill near the meat-cutting table. If the wolverine continued to walk up the hill 20 feet, it would almost be at my feet.

What to do when sitting on the Barren Lands at the top of a thinking hill minding your own business far from human beings, and a wolverine visits the camp and possibly wants to eat you?

There are times in life when fear sneaks up on you and jumps fast to hold your emotions. There are times you are so scared you don't know your mind is frozen from thought, just from the fact of being scared. There are also times in life when a dangerous confrontation tests your sense of survival, and you feel calm. I was fearful but instinctively knew nothing was going to happen to me.

However, I did wonder, "What do I do if it comes up to me and smells me? Please, God, don't let me feel the pain of being shredded to death. Don't let it eat me, God. Please, don't let it eat me, God. God, don't let it eat me." I don't know how many times I repeated the mantra.

My good ol' imagination worked overtime as it showed me how the attack might happen, and how I would attempt to fend off the animal about to take my life while I did my best to fight it off. I had to give my head a shake, because the animal of land and God's creation was, indeed, winding its way toward the meat-cutting stand. "I'll have to do my best to fight it. That's all I can do," I said under my breath, wondering if it heard me. I was convinced the best course of attack was the element of surprise.

I would sit very still, and when it came very close to me, I would hardly breathe. Only if it looked as though it was going to take a swipe at me would I reveal myself and jump out at it and scare the poop out of it.

If it would only go away.

But it didn't go anywhere, except past the meat-cutting stand, and now, past the meat-curing stage. I could see it quite clearly at the bottom of the hill.

It knew I was sitting at the top of the hill. It looked right into my eyes, and I, into its. I knew, it knew, I was there, because I had to blink a few times. It just stood at the bottom of the hill, looking at me.

It stood looking at me, and me at it, for at least three minutes, and I thought it was going to go away, but it began to walk up the snowy hillside. I looked at it but did not move. The wolverine took a few steps up the hill, and I thought it was going to paw a slow crawl to me. It sniffed in the direction of the meat-curing stand, looked up at me, and we looked into each other's eyes again. I wondered if it wondered what I was. I wondered if it felt any threat, from whatever it thought I was? It was about 12 feet from me.

Then, a most curious thing happened.

The wolverine turned and slowly ambled back to the meat-cutting table, around the cabin in the direction of where the dogs were tied, then walked past the dogs and through a clump of thick bush where the men bent plywood boards in the fall. I saw it turn once to look in my direction before it ambled up the small knoll behind the bush, and then it was gone.

And that is the truth, the whole truth and nothing but the truth, so help me God. It was a curious experience, and I believe, besides God, my naivety saved me. I thought about how the wolverine had looked into my eyes, and me into its eyes, and I didn't see or feel menace. It didn't growl or bare its teeth. What I thought most curious were the dogs. I watched the dogs when the wolverine walked on the outer rim of where all good protective dogs lay.

The dogs did not make a sound, did not bark, did not move. One dog stood and stretched and lay lazy in its snow mound, and all the dogs were oblivious to the wolverine.

"And these dogs are supposed to be my protectors?" I thought. "Why aren't they barking their crazy heads off? It's walking right past the dog circle." Not one dog acknowledged the presence of the wolverine.

I thought the wolverine would wake the sleeping dogs, or at least one dog, and fight it and eat it, but the dogs did nothing, and the wolverine did nothing except walk past the dogs. I thought the dogs would smell the wolverine. When I saw it shuffle over the hill, I thought, because I heard wolverines are smart animals, it might double back and attack me from behind. I waited a few minutes and surveyed the land. I was feeling the aftershock of a close encounter with a Barren Land wolverine and was afraid, yes, afraid, to move. "Maybe it's fooling me and will come running back through the bush at me when I am two feet from the main cabin door."

At the same time, I didn't want to sit in the thick snow in case I suddenly felt a big CLUCK on the back of my head. I know it sounds funny, but it was what I thought at the time.

"You gotta make a move," God, or something, said.

"But...but... but..." replied a voice, probably mine.

"No buts...just get moving..." is what I'm quite sure God said—I think it was God!

I ran as fast as thick snow allowed a person to run down the hill, past the meat-curing stage and meat-cutting table, past the short yard span to the cabin. Once in the cabin, I strung the rope over the nail on the frame of the outer door. Only when I was inside the main cabin did I become really, really, scared. All thoughts about wild animals breaking into the cabin were back in a flash and playing with my imagination. My afterthoughts were: "What if this happened, or what if that would have happened? Why didn't it come up to me? Why did it turn around and not come and fight me and eat me? Why didn't the dogs bark?"

Wolverines are wild, voracious, vicious, flesh-eating animals with a keen sense of smell. I've heard stories and read how wolverines are cunning, intelligent and seldom lose a fight against prey. A wolverine is a terror of the land, and no man, or woman, wants to tangle with one.

I was either very lucky with God's help or it was an old wolverine with cataracts and no sense of smell who thought I was a piece of rock and couldn't be bothered with a sweet young Barren Land bush bunny who smelled of rotten fish.

Maybe the rotten fish smell saved me. Maybe it didn't like rotten fish.

In the cabin, I waited and thought about how smart wolverines are and listened in the quiet afternoon to hear any sounds of a creature walking around the cabin or trying to push the door open. I mustered a brave façade to peer out the windows to look in all directions for small animals about to jump up at the window.

There were no wolverines or other animals in sight, and the dogs were still and quiet.

The dogs, however, did yelp, bark and jump at the approach of two sleighs loaded with wood. A huge pile was unloaded. During supper, I told the men of the experience. Richard looked at me and didn't say anything. Louison looked at me curiously and didn't say anything either. Both men looked at me, wanting to believe me, I thought, but didn't say a word.

The hot stove devoured the wood to avoid the cold weather from devouring the cabin. The stove-pipes steal cold air, and warm fire blows up the stovepipes, into the cold night air.

I lie in bed thinking about the experience, thanked God and thought about how each new day brings new experiences that soon become past experiences. I also thought about how new experiences, quite unbelievable experiences, dispel old myths and create new true stories and legends. I decided if I ever wrote a book about my time on the Barren Lands, I would call it *Myth of the Barrens*.

Every myth is based on reality. Years later, when I told the story, a friend said it was a ghost wolverine protector, and only I could see it. She said the wolverine didn't hurt me because it was my sign of a ghost protector. She said it was my protector, and I must have strong spiritual powers if it didn't harm me and if nothing else could see it, like the dogs. She said it would always protect me from anything trying to harm me. I believe in my Aboriginal spirituality and believed, and still believe, what she said to me.

I never saw a live wolverine again on the Barren Lands.

## 🦌 November 30, 1977–December 6, 1977 🦌

ON NOVEMBER 30, THE MEN WERE OFF TO OUTPOST camps. I chose to stay at the cabin. After I completed the chores, I didn't have much to do except knit, write in my diary and feed the dogs.

Well, it's good news day! Siskadoses is going to have pups. Richard said she should give birth at the end of December. He told Louison he hoped one of the pups will have a white strip under its chin and will be black, like his leader.

Richard brought her into the cabin because he said she would freeze, but she smelled so bad I told him she was not going to stay in the cabin. The smell of a stinky dog, combined with the heat and cooking, made me feel sick. Also, I didn't think it was healthy. He put her back outside, but once she had a taste of a warm cabin, she wanted more of the good life. He whipped her backside when she continually howled day and night but did not bring her back into the cabin.

Richard compromised by digging a cave in the deeply banked snow in the right angle corner near the cabin door where the addition was built. He lined it with a couple of caribou hides, and with the warmth from the cabin, she was content.

Between December 1 and December 8, we continued our trips to the outpost camps. The men skinned the fox, and I combed the fur of dead animals. The men were grateful, saying the results would be exchanged for plenty of money from southern auction marts. Richard shot a wolf and brought the skin to the cabin to flesh. Louison shot a *wolverine*. I wondered if it was the same wolverine I encountered. He said he shot it near the outpost camp we had travelled to by canoe earlier in the fall, where the caribou were shot crossing the jut of land. It may have been *my wolverine*, but I didn't think it was.